South of
Somewhere

Recipes and Stories from My
Life in South Africa, South Korea
& the American South

SIMON
ELEMENT

NEW YORK LONDON TORONTO
SYDNEY NEW DELHI

South of Somewhere

DALE GRAY

with Susan Choung

SIMON
ELEMENT

FOR MOM,
who always guides me
"home" by reminding
me of who I am.

Walking, I am listening to a deeper way. Suddenly all my ancestors are behind me. Be still, they say. Watch and listen. You are the result of the love of thousands.

—LINDA HOGAN

INTRODUCTION

SOUTH AFRICA

My journey begins in Wellington, South Africa, in a small, picturesque valley nestled at the foot of the Groenberg mountain on the outskirts of Cape Town. I was born the eldest of three girls, into a close-knit family that had been in the valley for generations. We lived modestly, moving around to other parts of South Africa for my dad's job. Dad was a machinist at a canning factory near Wellington, and Mom worked as a cash office clerk at the local grocery store. I attended Paarl Girls' High School, a semiprivate school in the neighboring town, all thanks to my mom, who believed that a good education was paramount. I learned about cooking in home economics class, where Mrs. Stoffberg said "Chef!" to me once after I shared a recipe with the other students. Her compliment felt sincere, and I began to wonder whether I could cook a little. It began with roasting chicken on weeknights to help Mom out, then I started serving up pasta like Nigella Lawson on the BBC Food channel. I fell in love with the olive oils produced in our valley, and one Christmas, I cooked up an olive oil–drenched feast inspired by Jamie Oliver. It was a disaster, and while Dad chuckled under his breath, my uncle Willie ate as if he were dining at a five-star restaurant. That was all the encouragement I needed to apply for a food science degree at Stellenbosch University, egged on by teachers who told me, "Don't worry about the money." To my surprise, I received a full scholarship and became one of the first girls in our family to attend college. During my third year of university, Mom and Dad decided to separate, and then it was just us women: Mom, myself, my younger sisters Aretha and Kim, and Grandma, who lived nearby. Together, we found joy in everyday life, and even when things got tough, a flicker of inner optimism saw us through.

On Sunday afternoons before we set the cake table for tea, Mom and I sat under the avocado tree in the yard of our rental and dreamed about all of life's possibilities. We dreamed far and wide, without any limitations to hold us back. I still remember my words as if they were spoken yesterday: "My future husband lives across the ocean, and that's where I'll start a family one day."

"Hold on to your dreams. Nobody can take that away from you, Daley," Mom would say as she sprinkled salt out of a shaker onto some snacking fruit.

Mom dreamed of living in a home that we owned, a new refrigerator to replace the old white KIC that had given up the ghost just a week prior, stability for Aretha and Kim, and a successful career for me after graduating from university. As the eldest, I felt compelled to do whatever I could to give Mom that kind of peace.

There's a way of life in South Africa, an African philosophy known as Ubuntu, and I've always understood it this way: Ubuntu is a sense of responsibility toward one's household, community, and society. In the spirit of Ubuntu, humanity is a quality we owe to each other. We share each other's burdens, and as a group, we aim to focus less on individual needs and more on the collective. If you pay close attention, Ubuntu can be seen in the smile from a stranger in passing, the way we share with each other when a neighbor needs a *potjie* pot, or a kid comes knocking with an empty cup in hand, asking, "Aunty, my mom asks if you have some sugar to borrow?" This philosophy had been ingrained in me since birth. Later in life, I realized how significant it was in my decision to leave. It was for the greater good of my family.

SOUTH KOREA

After graduating, I overheard some friends talk about teaching English in South Korea. Frustrated with the limited job options in South Africa, I decided to follow them without knowing one iota about the country. It was a life-altering move. You might think Korea couldn't be any more different from what I was used to—and there were certainly challenges—but growing up with the spirit of Ubuntu in South Africa helped me to understand the Confucian dynamics in Korea.

Other than the South Africans I knew, I wasn't aware of anyone who loved to cook, eat, and celebrate more than the people of South Korea. Even within just a few blocks, you could find a dozen restaurants, each specializing in something different, from raw seafood to grilled meats to braised family-style meals. Oftentimes, the restaurants would be packed to the brim with friends and families eating, drinking, and laughing. That togetherness and warmth while sharing a delicious meal was so genuine. When two people meet by chance, the common greeting is "Have you eaten today?" The question is mostly rhetorical, based on a deeper concern for them and their well-being; it's a way to show you care on the most basic level. I loved that so much!

Now, unable to spend Sunday afternoons with Mom, I'd take walks through Korean markets and ask questions with my limited Korean vocabulary. It was my mission to learn everything; and the people there were extremely generous with their knowledge. Time flew by, and I became a better cook every step of the way. Then one day in my fifth year, I met a handsome young American soldier who was serving his first tour of duty in Uijeongbu. After seven months of courtship, he asked me to be his wife and move back home with him. At that point, I knew nothing about America, except for the stereotypical characters shown on television. I had no idea what to expect.

SOUTHERN USA

My soldier was from the South. DJ was a gentleman who wanted me to meet his momma from whom I would learn to make his childhood favorites. He spoke endlessly about New Orleans and how growing up there exposed him to many different cultures and foods. He had joined the military hoping to make a better life for himself, and something about that resonated with me. Intrigued by it all, I decided that love would be enough to see me through another huge transition.

One sunny Sunday in September 2011, my soldier and I were wed beside a shimmering pond on his parents' property in Louisiana. His dad officiated the ceremony, DJ and I ate cake, and we danced the Electric Slide. His mom offered a brief introduction to collard greens, okra, and gumbo, then waved goodbye as we set off to our next duty station in El Paso. While the desert landscape of western Texas vaguely resembles certain areas in South Africa, the similarities stopped there. The difference in culture was stark, and adjusting to America proved to be much more challenging than anticipated. I felt hesitant to speak and couldn't shake off my habit of reflexively bowing to greet everyone! People laughed, and some rudely asked whether I had crossed the border from Mexico. I became reclusive as a result and started to wonder if I'd made the right decision to come here.

In the spirit of Ubuntu, I decided to put my all into doing the one thing I knew I was passionate about—cooking! DJ worked from nine to five while I spent my days preparing three-course meals every day of the week. I watched cooking shows, read cookbooks, and fumbled around the kitchen trying new techniques. While the food was good and I now had something to consume my time, it still wasn't filling the void I had in my heart for community. My next decision changed my life forever: I got on Instagram and created @thedaleyplate.

When I sat under that tree with my mother on Sundays, I never imagined that posting photos of my cooking online one day would open so many doors for me. In those early days, Instagram was like a lifeline, anchoring me to the larger family I longed for so much. I was firmly part of a global community that continued to grow as more food-loving people started making my recipes and relished stories of my journey, both the good parts and the bad.

It's been (and continues to be) an incredible journey I wouldn't trade for anything. When I do return to South Africa, Mom and I look back with gratitude and realize that all of our dreams have come to fruition now. Those aspirations shared under the tree propelled us forward, helped us overcome hurdles, and kept the fire in our hearts alive. Here in the sleepy town of Brookhaven, Mississippi, a vast ocean away from "home," I continue to keep the spirit of Ubuntu alive by cooking and sharing the food I grew up with, and the food inspired by each South that I've known.

EAST & WEST

So, What Is Cape Malay Food?

If you flip to the South African section of the 1967 edition of *The Cookbook of the United Nations* by Barbara Kraus, the official entries are "Bobotie," "Yellow Rice," "Sosaties," and "Peach Pickles." All these mouth-watering dishes come from the Cape Malay table. This is the food of my people. When I tell folks here in America about my background, the first question they ask me is "What is Cape Malay?" Often, the (rather blunt) follow-up question is "But why are you white?" I'm not. I'm a mix of a lot of things. To understand who the Cape Malays are now and why their cooking gives such a pertinent insight into the South African palate, we first need to delve into a little history.

By the middle of the seventeenth century, the Dutch East India Company, an agency founded in the Netherlands to protect trade in the Indian Ocean, realized that a pit stop was needed on the long sea route between home base and the spice-rich East Indies. This post became known as the Cape of Good Hope, and Jan van Riebeeck was appointed as the first leader of that settlement. His assignment was to build a hospital and cultivate a garden to provide passing ships with sustenance. He even erected a fort, the Castle of Good Hope, in the middle of what is now known as the "Parade," or city square in Cape Town.

This intrusion put the Europeans at odds with the Khoisan natives, and war became inevitable. To protect the fort and settlement, Van Riebeeck got reinforcements sent over in 1658 via Mardijkers, mercenaries and descendants of freed slaves from what is present-day

BOBOTIE, 149

GREEN BEAN STEW, 150

Indonesia (and a colony of the Dutch East India Company at the time). The Mardijkers are the ones credited with bringing the aromatic spices, which would later define the South African culinary landscape, during this relocation.

Meanwhile, the Dutch, fueled by a burning desire for a monopoly in the lucrative spice trade between the East and Europe, expanded their raids to the Spice Islands. The Portuguese, their main rivals, set up posts on the Malaysian Peninsula to guard their territory. In this tug of war for dominance, the Dutch established many outposts, from the Bay of Bengal to the southern Indian coast. From these points, highly skilled Indian, Malaysian, and Indonesian political exiles and slaves were brought to the Cape to establish a colony. These so-called "Malay" slaves were sought after and expensive because of their skilled labor in the households of wealthy Cape citizens. They were artisans, fishermen, needle-workers, and cooks, and the Cape's distinctive architecture remains a testament to their skill and craftsmanship.

The Cape Malays eventually intermarried with the other races who moved through the colony: the people of Madagascar, Mozambique, Angola, and Europe. Over the years, the identity of their descendants remains rooted in a rich culture—a colorful blend of Eastern and Western heritage. This commingling is immediately apparent in the cuisine, where the dishes can be sweet, savory, spicy, and salty all in one. For instance, in Bobotie (page 149), you'll find ground meat heady with curry powder and ground cloves, and sweet with raisins and chutney, baked under a rich, creamy custard fragrant with lemon leaves.

You might say the South Africans are kind of food obsessed. The humorous songs of my ancestors tell of new love and lost love but, above all, proclaim a love of food that almost borders on glorification. From the cradle to the grave, we celebrate every possible opportunity for tables buckling under the earth's abundance. Our favorite dishes showcase the alluring fruit from those orchards planted when the Cape was first established and are permeated with the exhilarating flavor of cloves, nutmeg, and pepper from the remote islands of our origin. By cooking the Cape Malay–inspired recipes in this book listed below, you can taste the subtle, sensual delights of Cape Town Malaysian food.

Bobotie, page 149   Green Bean Stew, page 150   Lamb Sosaties with Apricots, Bay & Onion, page 238   Pepper Jelly Salmon, page 184   District Six Apricot Chutney, page 89   Soetkoekies, page 263   Melktert, page 249   Festive Season Fruit & Nuts, page 69

KITCHEN STAPLES FOR ALL SENSES

koskas (kɔskas)
Noun (*Afrikaans*)

A wooden cupboard, usually with two doors, in which dry goods are kept.

These days it's common to see videos, guides, and how-tos online for the "perfect" pantry. Gorgeous glass jars with wooden tops sit neatly arranged on open shelving in kitchens for everyone to marvel at, but is that realistic? My pantry is the opposite of that, even though I tried to organize it a little for this book. The nervous laugh on my face in the photo in my kitchen is an indication that things aren't what they seem to be. As someone who works with food daily, I've mostly run out of space, and my kitchen, last renovated in the early 2000s, overflows with ingredients. If I try to list everything in my pantry here, you'd still be reading two years from now, so I'll spare you.

The guide that follows isn't extensive but will give you an idea of staples that I rely on grouped according to the six taste sensations—salty, spicy, sweet, sour, bitter, and umami.

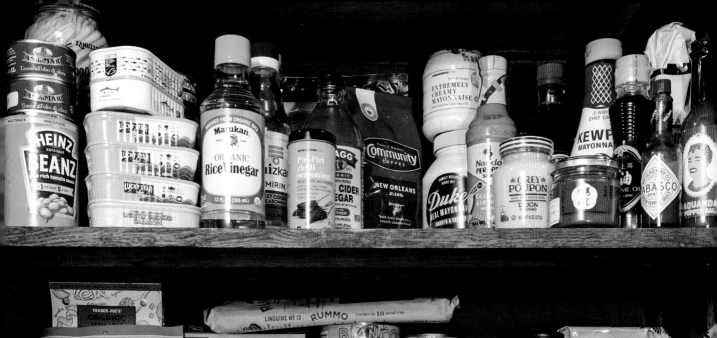

SALTY (SAVORY)

To make something taste good, you need a little more salt than you might think. There are many (understandable) reasons why people steer away from oversalting, but oftentimes, just a touch more can level up the outcome of a recipe. I use Morton **kosher salt** and season as I go, using about 1 teaspoon per pound for meat and freshwater fish, and about ½ teaspoon per pound for ocean fish, which are basically pre-seasoned with the ocean's salinity.

Throughout the book, recipes will ask you to season proteins in advance with kosher salt. This isn't because I want to waste your time or make cooking a chore—salting certain proteins ahead increases tenderness by denaturing (unraveling) the protein molecules that can sometimes cause the meat to be tough. This change in texture will pay off when it comes to eating your food. Wow, that food science degree I quit within the first year is really paying off!

I firmly believe that anything is made instantly more delicious with **flake salt**. A container of Maldon flake salt has earned a permanent place on our kitchen table, where we lightly sprinkle the crunchy, delicate crystals over both sweet and savory dishes right before serving.

SPICY

My favorite kind of spicy isn't coma-inducing explosive heat. While I'm no stranger to the fiery African bird's eye chile (piri-piri, from Mozambique), I've always preferred warm and fruity, mild and earthy, or rich and robust multilayered ingredients that provide both heat and flavor to my meals. These are a few staples in my kitchen that add both heat and flavor:

Black pepper

If salt is a necessity, then **black pepper** is a very good choice. Good quality, fresh, whole black peppercorns add complexity, heat, and sometimes sweet citrus notes, depending on their origin. I like Tellicherry peppercorns from India, bought in bulk and stored in an airtight container in the freezer to maintain freshness.

Chiles and chili powders

There are more than two hundred varieties of chiles ranging in size, color, and heat level. I grow bright green **serranos** and **jalapeños** in the summer and add them to recipes that need moderate heat. Generally speaking, the larger the chile, the milder it'll be. Fire-engine red **Thai bird's eye chile**, **piri-piri chile**, and **cayenne** are smaller and thus pack a punch. I use each of these fresh chiles in my cooking for a bright pop of heat instead of the slow burn of their dried counterparts. When selecting fresh chiles of any kind, look for those with vivid colors and firm skins.

When I run out of fresh chiles, I rely on **red pepper flakes** for their clean flavor that's versatile enough to use in a wide range of dishes. When I want a smokier heat, I reach for **chipotle chili powder**. For smokiness with fruitiness, I go for **ancho chili powder**. For heat with some sweetness, it's *gochugaru*, a Korean chili powder.

Curry powder

Curry powder isn't a single ingredient; rather, it's a general term for a blend of ground spices used to make curry, but not all curry powders are created equal. Once you find a blend that you like, stash it in the freezer to keep it fresh for longer. I squirrel away pounds of the good stuff after trips to Cape Town, purchased from Atlas Trading in District Six, an established Cape Malay community on the slopes of Table Mountain. The bags keep for a year in my freezer, but I ran out during the pandemic when travel wasn't an option. In my search for something equivalent from a US purveyor, I found the Vadouvan curry powder from The Spice House to be the closest to the fruity, mild blends used in South Africa. Alternatively, check Amazon or the international aisle of bigger grocery stores for Rajah curry and pick up the yellow box.

Hot sauce

There are as many kinds of hot sauce as there are stars in the sky. I like Nando's **garlic peri-peri**, a South African hot sauce with added garlic and herbs. It has a deeper flavor than the vinegary, sharp **Tabasco** that my husband, DJ, loves. I add splashes of hot sauce directly into food during cooking and finish meals with a few drops when needed. A dash of hot sauce is just what's missing in eggs, tacos, and soups—even in a bowl of vanilla ice cream, if you're feeling adventurous!

Gochujang

Many years ago in South Korea, I had my first taste of this fermented chili paste. For generations, the South Korean people have expertly crafted **gochujang** from chilies that are left out to dry in the summer months. They are ground into a paste with salt, ground rice, and fermented soybeans, then packed into *onggi*, earthenware crocks that are kept outside while the paste ferments. Making gochujang is an art, and I wouldn't dare attempt it myself. Thankfully it is available in most grocery stores as Korean food has become more popular in the US. When shopping for gochujang, look at the ingredient list and choose something with the least amount of additives for a superior flavor. I prefer gochujang that is milder, darker in color, and has a spreadable consistency. It can be kept in the refrigerator for months at a time and gives any soup or stew extra depth. At first, you taste an earthiness, then fiery heat and a fruitiness toward the end. I have to say, it took me a while to come around to it, but now I add this chili paste to any and everything because you don't know the value of something until you're on the other side of the world.

Spicy ingredients of a different kind

Prepared horseradish and **horseradish powder**, and dry **English mustard** all deliver heat with a nose-clearing pungency. I like to add any of these to any savory meals that require a little je ne sais quoi.

RECIPES TO TRY

Smoky Chicken-Topped Sweet Potatoes, page 107   Lamb Sosaties with Apricots, Bay & Onion, page 184, Bobotie, 149   Garlic Peri-Peri Roast Chicken, page 124   Shrimp Tacos with Peri-Peri Yogurt Sauce, page 95   Herby Horseradish Mashed Potatoes, page 139

SWEET

The land in South Africa is blessed with tasty crops, so we have a long history of incorporating sweet fruit and chutneys into savory recipes. It's not that I have a huge sweet tooth, but I like some sugar with my salt. Simply put, I add a touch of sweetness to this and that because that's how my mother, and her mother before her, cooked.

Sugars and syrups

I use these interchangeably throughout the book and in my everyday cooking. **Maple syrup** is my first choice because it dissolves easily. Maple syrup is made from the sap of sugar maple, black maple, or red maple trees. When using the buttery, naturally vanilla-flavored syrup in cooking, I buy whichever kind is most affordable because the goal is only to amplify sweetness. If the flavor of maple syrup is important (when making desserts or coffee), I buy it from smaller artisans with a variety of cool flavors. Try Bushwick Kitchen's gingerbread maple syrup in the fall! I buy local Mississippi **honey** from the Piggly Wiggly (a grocery store) down the road and keep both **white** and **light brown sugar**, **sorghum syrup**, and **monk fruit sweetener** in stock for everyday cooking. The latter is a great naturally sugar-free alternative without an artificial aftertaste.

Jam, preserves, and fruit

The canned food factory shop just a few blocks away from my childhood home was my parents' go-to stop when money was tight in the late nineties. There, shoppers could grab a box and fill it up with dented and rejected cans at a discounted price. They were more affordable than store-bought, with the only caveat being no labels to identify what was inside! While cooking dinner and pressed for time, Mom would ask my sisters and I to open a can of peas, beans, or carrots that she needed quickly, and we'd carefully inspect those dented cans to guess before trying our luck with the electric opener. It went from fun to frustrating quickly after our third and fourth attempts only seemed to produce more cans of mixed **fruit jam**. Thankfully, Mom always found ways to use the sweet stuff. I keep one or two jars of jam or **preserves** on hand for desserts, marinades, and my District Six Apricot Chutney (page 263), a sweet and sour condiment used for dipping and cooking. Dried fruit like **apricots**, **raisins**, and **cranberries** keep forever in the freezer and their sweetness pairs well with savory ingredients.

RECIPES TO TRY

Burrata with Peaches, Honeycomb, & Pecan Dukkah, page 56   Bobotie, page 149
Not an Italian Grandma's Cheesy Lasagna, page 142   Shebashuka, page 188
Lamb Sosaties with Apricots, Bay and Onion, page 184   Pepper Jelly Salmon, page 89
Skillet Jezebel Chicken with Peach & Herb Salad, page 110   District Six Apricot Chutney, page 263
Tomato & Onion Grilled Cheese Sandwiches (Braaibroodjies), page 219

SOUR (ACIDITY)

For some, the word *sour* conjures up lip-puckering, not-so-great memories, but when it comes to balancing flavors and adding brightness, nothing does it quite like a hint of acidity. During my college years I tried cooking pork chops for the first time, with vinegar and apples, and my roommate nearly passed out before she set her plate to the side. To avoid too much acidity the key is definitely moderation, and using ingredients like vinegar and citrus to enhance other flavors rather than to dominate them.

Vinegar

Vinegar is a staple that lasts forever in the pantry, and I keep a small collection on hand for a few different applications. Each kind varies in acidity, and the percentage is usually written on the label. For recipes like vinaigrettes that require less acidity and a more balanced, rounded flavor, I prefer **white balsamic vinegar**. The sharp, bracing tang of **white distilled vinegar** is ideal for pickling and preserving, but I also use it in savory recipes to cure and tenderize meat. Fruity **apple cider vinegar** is my vinegar of choice for sauces, and it pairs perfectly with pork or brassicas, and **unseasoned rice wine vinegar** is indispensable when it comes to any of the Korean recipes in this book.

Citrus

At any given time, a bowl of **lemons** and **limes** sit and wait on my kitchen table. I go through that bowl rapidly because most meals that I cook must be finished with citrus for a bright, fresh touch. In Cloudy Day Lentil Soup (page 223), the addition of lemon is so important that I cried one day after realizing I'd run out. It's that serious. Keep them handy, and if possible, buy unwaxed lemons for zesting or scrub them really well under warm running water before using.

RECIPES TO TRY

Skillet Jezebel Chicken with Peach & Herb Salad, page 110   Wild Rice Bowls with Roasted Beets, Goat Cheese & Preserved Lemon Drizzle, page 215   Cloudy Day Lentil Soup, page 223   Birthday Beef Cheeks with Preserved Lemon Gremolata, page 139   Mom's Red Beans with Smoked Turkey, page 129   Chicken with Saucy Rosemary Beans, page 126   Garlic & Herb Chicken Flattie, page 119   Pasta with Scallops & Lemony Garlic Butter, page 93   Crab Cakes Piccata, page 100

BITTER

At first glance, I'm sure the word bitter doesn't sound at all appealing. I don't know if most people would agree, but ingredients with an innately bitter taste helps to balance out the flavors of a meal. I rely on these ingredients to create harmony when needed:

Olive oil

The flavor of **olive oil** varies depending on the region it comes from, and this is one ingredient where quality matters. I seek out artisans who produce small-batch olive oil for finishing dishes, and the grassy olive oils produced in California for cooking.

Olives

Big olive fan here! Their briny, slightly bitter flavor shines on their own as a snack and in many recipes in this book. **Castelvetrano olives**, a green Spanish variety with a meaty texture and a buttery, milder taste, are my first choice for salads. I recommend them to anyone on the fence about olives as a gateway to the more flavor-forward black **Kalamata** or **Koroneiki olives**.

Bitter greens

My mother always says, "You need something green on that plate!" and I tend to agree with her. I include bitter greens like **watercress**, **arugula**, **radicchio** and slightly bitter **cruciferous vegetables** in side dishes and salads often because they have the ability to cut through richer mains.

Fresh and dried herbs

Cooking with herbs like **oregano**, **thyme**, **rosemary**, **cilantro**, and **parsley** adds a floral, herbaceous liveliness to recipes that can't be beat. My first choice for dishes that require minimal cooking or garnishes will always be fresh because of the aroma and visual appeal of the herbs, but swapping out fresh for dried herbs matters less for stews, soups, or sauces. If you prefer to use dried herbs instead, use half the amount called for in a recipe because dried herbs are more potent than fresh. To store fresh herb bundles and keep them looking their best, wrap them in a damp paper towel, then place in an airtight container or zip-top bag and refrigerate.

RECIPES TO TRY

Pepper Jelly Salmon, page 89   Chicken with Chorizo & Olives, by Request, page 115

Chilled Beef Tenderloin with Tonnato Sauce, page 158   Forgotten Greens Mac & Cheese, page 204

UMAMI

It may be last on the list, but that doesn't make umami any less important than the more familiar senses. In fact, it's probably the one I most appreciate. These ingredients add that little something extra to food, and make people ask, "What *is* that (pleasant) flavor?"

Umami spices and sprinkles

Throughout this book, you'll notice whole spices, freshly ground spices, and store-bought spice blends in ingredient lists. I make use of many dry spices and blends and consider them essential when it comes to building flavor during the cooking process.

SMOKED PAPRIKA is the superior spice! If I could only have one spice, a great jar of smoked paprika would be it. Buy excellent quality, fresh smoked paprika for best results. Look for deeply smoky **Spanish paprika (pimenton)** online or in well-stocked grocery stores.

For some of the South African–inspired recipes, having fresh **clove**, **nutmeg**, **cinnamon**, **ground ginger**, and **mustard seeds** on hand is a good idea. For the rest, I recommend **Cavender's**, a Greek American staple; **Cajun seasoning** (I like Slap Ya Mama); store-bought **lemon pepper** seasoning (Lawry's or Frontier Co-Op make good ones); **Old Bay**; **Japanese furikake**, a blend of dried seaweed, sesame seeds, sugar, and various other ingredients that can be found online or at most Asian markets (JFC Kimchi Furikake is my favorite one!); and **Creole Seasoning** (page 256), my homespun Creole blend with extra dried herbs.

Other umami ingredients

ANCHOVIES: are preserved in three ways: in oil, vinegar, or salt. When I make Chilled Beef Tenderloin with Tonnato Sauce (page 158), I use **anchovies** packed in olive oil, and my friends can never believe that a sauce with anchovies can pair well with beef. Their flavor isn't apparent, but if you left them out, you'd notice immediately. I could eat tinned anchovies packed in olive oil straight out of the can, and often do. To eat them as-is, in salads, or with pickles, I like Ortiz or Agostino Recca anchovies packed in olive oil. For general cooking, any kind packed in olive oil will do.

WORCESTERSHIRE SAUCE: This vinegar-based fermented sauce includes salty anchovies, sour tamarind, sweet molasses, onion, garlic, and spices. My dad always put a bottle on the table when serving soup, and my sisters and I went to town with that **Worcestershire sauce**, often testing the limits of just how much was too much. I guess the flavor that kept compelling us to add more was umami! I like the tang of Lea & Perrins Worcestershire sauce in soups and stews and keep a bottle of the low-sodium version on my dinner table for anyone who needs more.

Soy sauce and **miso paste** are common ingredients in modern kitchens, so I don't feel they need much explaining. I will, however, recommend trying different kinds of both. There's more variety on offer at bigger Asian markets or grocery stores like H Mart. I mostly use **white miso paste** with bonito—cured, smoked fish that gives any broth, soup, or roast a hefty injection of umami. **Parmesan cheese**, **fish sauce**, **dashi powder**, and **tomato paste** are all worth their weight in gold as well.

RECIPES TO TRY

Nuoc Cham Chicken Wings with Papaya & Peanuts, page 52

Soul-Satisfying Fish Cake Dinner (Eomuk Bokkeum), page 86   Ground Beef Bulgogi Bowls, page 154

Miso-Braised Pork Shoulder, page 172   Okonomiyaki Cabbage "Steaks," page 212

LIVING THAT LOW-WASTE LIFE

Sometimes a dish is bland and then it needs salt. Other times reducing waste can look like using up every ingredient in the refrigerator before they aren't salvageable. Those are typically less challenging problems to solve. Here are some ideas for less waste when things are particularly challenging in the kitchen:

It's burnt!

Try again next time, but remember that you control the heat. When you start to feel a bit flustered during the cooking process, just lower the heat and think things through. Pull the food off the heat completely to ease any pressure, then give yourself some time to regroup. We could all use a little more grace when it comes to how we treat ourselves. When I gently burn some things that are still pretty edible, I like to quote the Argentine chef Francis Mallmann, who said, "Burnt is also a flavor." So there's that.

It's undercooked!

Cooking temperatures and times vary so greatly by height above sea level, that it's impossible to have 100 percent accuracy across the board. If you find that something needs more time, keep cooking over a lower heat longer than called for and taste in five minute increments until you're completely satisfied. I've always found that an instant-read thermometer is the absolute best way to determine doneness when cooking meat.

It's overcooked!

In my ninth grade home economics class, I learned the French word *réchauffé*, which means to create a different meal with leftovers. Growing up poor, you become a master at this. When our very well-to-do teacher Mrs. Stoffberg taught us that word, I thought to myself, "Wow, there's a word for how we live every day?" The truth is, we learned to be masters at repurposing leftovers out of necessity. I'm very good at réchauffé, ma'am. Here are some no-recipe ideas that might help you repurpose a meal that might not have worked out today:

GOT LEFTOVERS?

Chicken

Lemony Chicken Salad: In a medium bowl, stir together 4 cups shredded, cooked chicken, ¼ cup mayonnaise, ¼ cup sour cream or plain yogurt, the grated zest and juice of 1 small lemon, 2 tablespoons chopped fresh herbs, 1 tablespoon finely chopped kosher dill pickle, and 1 tablespoon finely chopped red onion until well combined. Season to taste with kosher salt and freshly ground black pepper, and serve, or refrigerate in an airtight container for up to 3 days.

Rice

Jook: Combine equal parts cooked rice and chicken stock in a large pot. Add as much finely minced garlic and chopped fresh ginger as you like. Simmer over medium heat until the rice has completely broken down, then drizzle with sesame oil and sprinkle with toasted sesame seeds. Serve with leftover roasted vegetables, Easy Mak Kimchi (page 260), or store-bought kimchi.

Beans and legumes

Let me just say that overcooked does *not* mean burnt when it comes to beans and legumes. This is one of the few exceptions to the previous Francis Mallmann quote (see also bacon, page 39) because there is nothing worse than a scorched pot of beans. If your beans are just overcooked, try making refried beans by cooking 4 strips of chopped bacon in a skillet, then add 1 diced onion, 4 finely minced garlic cloves, 1 teaspoon ground cumin, and 4 cups of your overcooked beans. Add enough chicken stock to cover and simmer until the liquid has completely evaporated. Mash with a fork and serve it with breakfast the next day.

Eggs

Make some fried rice that works with hard-boiled eggs or fried eggs (I've overcooked them and set aside because they weren't Instagram-worthy, and made a whole other egg for the aesthetics at times!). Chop up one or two eggs and add to the Shrimp Fried Rice, Cape Town Style (page 99).

Steak

I use unevenly cooked steaks left over from date night to top a bowl of Korean instant ramen. It's my husband's favorite late-night snack. Slice the steak very thinly against the grain; the thinner, the better. It's already overcooked, so you don't want to chomp on big tough chunks of shoe leather. Combine 1 tablespoon soy sauce with 1 teaspoon honey and 1 teaspoon of any red chili paste in a small bowl for every 8 ounces of leftover steak and set aside. Heat 1 tablespoon avocado oil in a cast-iron skillet over medium-high heat. Add the steak and cook until crisp. You might get nervous, but continue to cook until you see some light charring, about 2 minutes. Lower the heat to medium and pour in the prepared sauce. Cook and stir until the meat has soaked up the sauce. Serve it over your favorite instant ramen (we like Ottogi Mild or any flavor from Nongshim) with leftover vegetables on top, if desired.

Pasta

I just want to remind you that this is a no-judgment zone and things happen. When we were kids, we overcooked pasta on purpose so that it would *really* stick to the ceiling, then land on an unsuspecting sibling's head when they least expected it. Priceless memories. Add overcooked pasta to the All About the Feta Frittata (page 197), or make this easy cacio e pepe egg dish! Place 2 strips of chopped bacon in a skillet over medium-high heat and cook until the bacon is no longer opaque, 2 to 3 minutes. I hope that you remember what I wrote on page 37 about burning things and will reduce the heat if you need to. Add the well-drained overcooked pasta and cook until any liquid has evaporated. Make wells in the middle and drop an egg into each one. Cook with a lid on until the pasta is crispy on the bottom and the egg yolks set. Sprinkle over some Parmesan and freshly ground black pepper, then enjoy!

Vegetables

I think many of us can relate to the very, very grayish green beans that graced our plates as kids. Well, that is, if you're an elder millennial or older, like me. Nothing was worse than hearing my dad say "eat your vegetables," knowing that the vegetables looked so sad. This is why I prefer a method I picked up from America's Test Kitchen (see Haricots Verts with Burst Tomatoes & Cannellini Beans, page 224) that ensures even, bright green beans. If you've let any greens go for too long, chop them up finely then add a generous amount of fresh lemon juice, olive oil, and season to taste with kosher salt, then spoon it over cooked proteins.

COME FOR A BRAAI

If there was a golden thread tying South African people worldwide together, a *braai* would be it. We even dedicated a national holiday to the pastime, Heritage Day aka National Braai Day, every year on the twenty-fourth of September.

The fire stands at the very center of our social interaction, and we are as stoked as goats to chop wood for a braai year-round, come rain or shine. I've seen South Africans braaiing in -15 degree (Fahrenheit!) Alaskan weather, drinking Springbokkies (peppermint liqueur and marula fruit shots; page 45) while smiling for selfies to share on social media. Everyone understands that the braai is worth it.

I consider it to be a moment to slow down and celebrate loved ones with delicious food touched by fire. While my husband, DJ, a gas-grilling American, doesn't quite get the appeal of smelling like a campfire, I embrace the braai's familiar comfort, and wait a day or two before washing the smoke out of my curls.

Although Mississippi is more than 8,000 miles away from my homeland, I keep the fire burning any way I can to feel connected to my culture—even if my braai is just a janky fire pit from Walmart.

Anything you'd grill can be cooked over a wood fire. Some of my favorite recipes include Crispy Grilled Lamb Chops with Fresh Chakalaka Salad (page 176), *Braaibroodjies* (page 219), and Grilled Bavette Steak with Watermelon & Halloumi Salad (page 146).

SOUTH OF SOMEWHERE

Crispy Grilled Lamb Chops with
Fresh Chakalaka Salad, 176

Peppermint Liqueur Shot (Springbokkie)

Serves 1 This classic South African shot got its name after the South Africa national rugby team (the Springboks) won the World Cup in 1995, and mimics the green and gold colors of South African national uniforms. It's a real conversation starter in our home, and the first drink we whip out when getting ready for a braai. I know that a peppermint-flavored drink might lead you to believe that it'll taste like toothpaste; on the contrary, the creamy Amarula liqueur provides a beautiful balance. If you cannot find Amarula cream liqueur, any Irish cream liqueur makes a great substitute.

1 ounce green crème de menthe, chilled

1 ounce Amarula cream liqueur, chilled

In a shot glass, add the crème de menthe. Carefully pour the Amarula over the back of a spoon and into the shot glass to create a layered effect. Serve immediately.

NUOC CHAM CHICKEN WINGS
WITH PAPAYA & PEANUTS, 52

one

SNACKS & DRINKS

Peppadew & Gouda Pimento Cheese

Serves 8 (about 2 cups)   I've been told that if there was one Southern recipe I absolutely needed to master, it would be pimento cheese. In this spin on the classic, I use sweet and spicy pickled Peppadew peppers (instead of the usual pimiento peppers) and Gouda cheese, both staples in South Africa. The result is a creamy, mildly flavored pimento cheese with a touch of heat and slightly herbaceous undertones thanks to the oregano. The herbs and cheese pair perfectly with tomatoes and form the base of the galette on page 206, but it's equally as good as a snack with crackers, crunchy vegetables, pickles, and charcuterie. It won the stamp of approval from many of my Southern friends, and my husband thinks it tastes like pizza, which is a big win, in my opinion.

4 ounces cream cheese, softened

4 ounces extra-sharp Cheddar cheese, shredded

4 ounces Gouda cheese, shredded

½ cup jarred Peppadew peppers, finely chopped, plus 2 tablespoons pickling liquid (see Note)

¼ cup mayonnaise or whole-milk plain Greek yogurt

½ teaspoon garlic powder

½ teaspoon smoked paprika

¼ teaspoon dried oregano

⅛ teaspoon cayenne pepper

Assorted crackers, sliced vegetables, fruit, charcuterie, and/or nuts, for serving

In a large bowl, combine the cream cheese, Cheddar, Gouda, peppers and pickling liquid, mayonnaise, garlic powder, paprika, oregano, and cayenne. Stir until evenly mixed. You can serve the pimento cheese right away with any of the accompaniments, or refrigerate it in an airtight container for up to 5 days.

Note
You can replace Peppadew peppers with hot or mild pickled cherry peppers or ¼ cup diced pimientos in equal quantities.

Kumquat Pepper Jelly Goat Cheese Cups

Makes 4 to 5 (4-ounce) cups   This sweet and mildly spicy appetizer is a delicious treat to stash in the freezer for those days when the only snack you want is something creamy, cheesy, and bright. When I was a kid, my mom would portion and freeze most of our snacks or food soon after buying them in an effort to reduce as much waste as possible (it was really to prevent us from eating it all in one go). She bought huge blocks of Gouda cheese and shredded it herself, dividing it into containers to be thawed for school lunch sandwiches throughout the month. She shredded chubs of bologna with a box grater for the same reason. I learned to apply this kind of sensibility to my everyday life as a result, and it's no more apparent when taking a glance at the huge selection of cheese in my freezer.

These freezer-friendly goat cheese cups are inspired by the classic cream cheese and pepper jelly appetizer typically served with saltines or Ritz crackers here in the South. I often find myself with a basket of fresh kumquats from a neighbor, and my first reaction is always to preserve them by making a pepper jelly that can be enjoyed year-round. The jewel-toned, marmalade-like jelly is spooned into cups then topped with tangy goat cheese that can be tipped over and served with your favorite crackers at a moment's notice.

8 ounces kumquats, sliced then seeded

1 medium jalapeño, seeded and finely diced

2 tablespoons finely diced red bell pepper

⅓ cup distilled white vinegar

½ teaspoon chopped fresh rosemary needles

½ teaspoon kosher salt

1¼ cups sugar, divided

½ teaspoon powdered pectin

1 pound fresh goat cheese, softened

Crackers, for serving

1   In a large pot, combine the kumquats, jalapeño, bell pepper, vinegar, rosemary, salt, and 1 cup of the sugar. Bring to a rolling boil over medium heat, then lower the heat to medium-low. Cook, stirring occasionally, until the kumquat rinds are soft, about 15 minutes.

2   In a small bowl, stir together the pectin with the remaining ¼ cup sugar. Add to the jelly and cook over medium heat, stirring occasionally, until the jelly reaches 220°F on an instant-read thermometer, about 2 minutes. Remove from the heat and let cool to room temperature.

3   In each cup, spoon 2 tablespoons of the jelly, then top with enough goat cheese to fill the cup. Smooth the tops with the back of a spoon or silicone spatula. Refrigerate until the cheese is firm, about 30 minutes.

4   Tip one of the cups out onto a cheese board, and serve with your favorite crackers. Tightly wrap the remaining cups in plastic wrap and freeze until ready to thaw and serve. The goat cheese cups are best when thawed in the refrigerator overnight but can also be thawed at room temperature for 30 minutes before serving to knock out the chill.

Note

If you'd rather not delve into the world of homemade jelly, it's not a requirement in any way. Feel free to take advantage of the ever-expanding selection of artisanal jams and preserves, and choose your own adventure! Some of my favorites include yuzu marmalade, marionberry preserves, and leftover cranberry sauce with orange zest in the fall.

Heads-up

You'll need 4-ounce freezer-safe cups for this recipe. I love to repurpose the plastic sauce containers with lids when we order takeout.

SOUTH OF SOMEWHERE

Nuoc Cham Chicken Wings with Papaya & Peanuts

Serves 4   Upon my arrival to the American South, I felt lucky when I learned that New Orleans had a vibrant Vietnamese community with a variety of incredible restaurants. The refreshing flavors always do wonders to liven a weary palate, which inspires me to break free of any dreadful cooking ruts (and there are many).

When I can't make the trip to New Orleans, I try to channel those vibrant flavors into dishes, like these chicken wings. I season the wings with a marinade inspired by *nuoc cham*, the tangy, spicy, and sweet Vietnamese dipping sauce usually served alongside spring rolls or drizzled over noodles and steamed fish dishes. Whereas Vietnamese fish sauce wings, *cánh gà chiên nuoc mam*, are typically deep-fried, I quickly broil mine until crispy and caramelized.

Looping back to Mississippi, I garnish the umami-rich wings with roasted peanuts that I pick up from Brookway Market Basket, a mom-and-pop produce stand with a big barrel for roasting peanuts year-round. Ripe papaya adds sweetness, some fresh herbs add brightness, and a few juicy IPAs alongside can never hurt.

1   In a large bowl, stir together the lemongrass, chile, garlic, fish sauce, lime juice, maple syrup, and salt. Add the chicken wings, toss until evenly coated, then cover and refrigerate for at least 3 hours and up to overnight. Remove from the refrigerator 30 minutes before cooking.

2   Preheat the oven to broil with a rack positioned 10 inches from the broiler. Line a large rimmed sheet pan with aluminum foil.

3   Transfer the wings to the prepared sheet pan, spreading into an even layer, and broil, turning occasionally, until crisp, sticky, and golden brown, 15 to 20 minutes. Broiling the wings keeps them very juicy and takes less time than baking, but keep an eye on the wings after 15 minutes—the marinade tends to brown quickly.

4   Transfer the wings to a large platter with the papaya. Scatter the peanuts, mint, and Thai basil on top, then serve immediately.

1 lemongrass stalk, trimmed and minced

1 fresh Fresno chile, seeded and finely chopped

4 garlic cloves, minced

2 tablespoons fish sauce

2 tablespoons fresh lime juice

1 tablespoon pure maple syrup or light brown sugar

1 teaspoon kosher salt

2 pounds chicken wing drumettes and flats

¼ small papaya, peeled and cut into 3-inch-long slices

½ cup unsalted roasted peanuts

¼ cup loosely packed fresh mint leaves

¼ cup loosely packed fresh Thai basil leaves

Mustard & Marcona Almond-Dressed Eggs

Serves 4 to 6 While traditional Southern deviled eggs are quite delicious, this take on the classic offers an easy, mayo-free alternative that you can pull together last minute because there's no dainty yolk scooping to be done. Friends and family who stop by for a quick visit on the front porch love the unexpected lemony flavor and become goggly-eyed the minute I walk out with a tray from the kitchen. Sometimes, random baskets of local eggs appear at my door as a thank-you, and I feel like the ultimate Southern hostess. I top the boiled egg halves with a punchy mustard-based dressing that has a not-so-secret ingredient: Marcona almonds, meatier Spanish almonds with a buttery flavor and gentler crunch than the classic variety. The nuts add just the right amount of texture to perfectly contrast the jammy yolks.

6 large eggs

¼ cup roughly chopped Marcona almonds (see Note)

2 tablespoons Dijon mustard

1 tablespoon honey

1 tablespoon finely chopped fresh parsley

1 teaspoon fresh lemon juice

1 teaspoon chopped fresh chives, for garnish

Fresh dill fronds, for garnish (optional)

1 Bring a large saucepan of salted water to a rapid boil over medium-high heat. Use a ladle or slotted spoon to gently lower the eggs into the boiling water, then reduce the heat to medium. Cook the eggs for 7 minutes for jammy yolks, and 1 to 2 minutes longer for firmer yolks. Meanwhile, fill a large bowl with ice water.

2 Drain the eggs and submerge them in the ice bath until cooled. Gently tap each egg on the counter to crack them all over, then peel, occasionally dipping them in the water to rinse off any shell as you peel.

3 Using a sharp knife, cut each egg in half lengthwise, wiping the knife clean with a damp paper towel after each cut (not a must, but they'll look much neater this way). Transfer the egg halves to a serving platter.

4 In a small bowl, stir together the almonds, Dijon mustard, honey, parsley, and lemon juice until well combined. Spoon about 1 teaspoon of the mustard dressing on top of each egg half, and garnish with the chives and dill fronds, if desired. Serve immediately.

Note

If Marcona almonds aren't available, you can transform raw almonds to make them more tender and buttery. In a medium bowl, combine ¼ cup whole raw almonds, ¼ teaspoon kosher salt, and 1 cup of boiling water. Cover and let sit for 8 to 24 hours. The almonds will plump up and their skins will loosen, at which point you can decide whether to remove the skin or not. To do so, simply drain and rinse the almonds, then pat dry with paper towels. Grab a handful and rub them together in your palms. The skins should flake right off. Chop the almonds and use immediately.

Fun Twist

To spin this recipe into a simple salad, arrange the cooked egg halves on plated tender greens like baby spinach, arugula, or a spring mix, then add a few slices of prosciutto, country ham, or chopped cooked bacon before topping with croutons and spooning the mustard sauce over.

Burrata with Peaches, Honeycomb & Pecan Dukkah

Serves 2   Peaches and cream but make it fancy! Straddling the line between an appetizer and a dessert, and between sweet and savory, this is such a decadent way to begin or end a meal. It takes almost no time to prepare because the peaches are served fresh, the best way to experience them in peak peach season if you ask me. While I think they already are a treat as-is, sometimes special occasions call for a little luxury. When I was younger, canned yellow cling peach halves in syrup were served with a spoonful of sweetened Nestle dessert cream, a no-frills finish to a rather large Sunday meal. Now, I'm more inclined to eat my after-dinner peaches with local honeycomb, creamy *burrata*, and dukkah, a savory blend of nuts and spices. The dukkah adds a little salt and crunch to contrast the milky richness of the cream-filled mozzarella cheese and sweet fruit. While hazelnuts are more typical in Egypt where dukkah originates, the pecans in Mississippi need using, so I make that substitution in my blend. Depending on what's growing, I finish the plates with a handful of fresh herbs and a silky pour of olive oil.

2 very ripe peaches, halved, pitted, and cut into wedges

2 (4-ounce) burrata balls

4 ounces honeycomb, cut into thin slices or broken into chunks (see Note)

1 tablespoon Pecan Dukkah (recipe follows) or store-bought dukkah

2 tablespoons extra-virgin olive oil

Fresh herb leaves (any combination of mint, basil, or thyme), for garnish

Divide the peaches between two plates. Tear each burrata ball into chunks by hand, working over the peaches and gently laying them down on top of the peaches. Top with the honeycomb, sprinkle with the dukkah, and drizzle with the olive oil. Garnish with the herbs, and serve immediately.

Note
You can drizzle each plate with 1 tablespoon of honey or maple syrup in lieu of honeycomb.

PECAN DUKKAH

Makes about ⅔ cup

½ cup raw pecan halves

1 tablespoon toasted sesame seeds

2 teaspoons whole coriander seeds

1 teaspoon cumin seeds

1 teaspoon fennel seeds

½ teaspoon kosher salt

¼ teaspoon freshly ground black pepper

In a small skillet over medium-low heat, cook the pecans, stirring occasionally, until fragrant and lightly toasted, about 3 minutes. Add the sesame, coriander, cumin, and fennel seeds, and continue to toast, stirring occasionally, until the seeds start to pop, about 1 minute more. Immediately transfer the toasted nuts and seeds to a food processor. Add the salt and pepper, and pulse until coarsely ground, 15 to 18 pulses. Serve right away, or let cool and store in an airtight container at room temperature for up to 3 months.

Porch Party Shrimp with Mississippi Comeback Sauce

Serves 4   Here in Mississippi, shrimp is often served with a side of comeback sauce, a mildly spicy, piquant sauce otherwise known as the house dressing of the state because it's such an everyday staple. As the story goes, it was first created by a Greek restaurant owner up the road in Jackson and got its quirky name because people kept coming back for more. Similar to a New Orleans remoulade, my favorite version of Mississippi comeback sauce makes an excellent dip for fresh seafood. This easy sharing platter is loaded with oven-roasted jumbo Gulf shrimp for maximum sauce shoveling and, sometimes, raw vegetables, which my other half eats begrudgingly. Though not a must, serve with whichever vegetables or sides you prefer, and make this recipe your own wonderful creation. The shrimp can be served warm or chilled depending on the season, and any leftovers make for an excellent late-night snack.

MISSISSIPPI COMEBACK SAUCE
½ cup mayonnaise (I'm a Duke's fan)

2 tablespoons buttermilk

1 tablespoon ketchup or chili sauce (such as Heinz)

2 teaspoons Creole or stone-ground mustard

1 teaspoon Worcestershire sauce

1 teaspoon Tabasco sauce, or any vinegar-based hot sauce, plus more to taste

½ teaspoon smoked paprika

½ teaspoon garlic powder

SHRIMP
1 pound jumbo shrimp (21 to 25 shrimp; see Note), peeled and deveined, tails left intact

2 tablespoons extra-virgin olive oil

Grated zest and juice of 1 small lemon

1 teaspoon garlic powder

½ teaspoon kosher salt

⅛ teaspoon cayenne pepper

1   TO MAKE THE COMEBACK SAUCE, in a small bowl, stir together the mayonnaise, buttermilk, ketchup, mustard, Worcestershire sauce, hot sauce, smoked paprika, and garlic powder until well combined. Cover and refrigerate until ready to use.

2   TO MAKE THE SHRIMP, preheat the oven to 425°F with a rack in the center position.

3   In a large bowl, toss the shrimp with the olive oil, lemon zest and juice, garlic powder, salt, and cayenne until the shrimp is evenly coated.

4   On a large rimmed sheet pan, arrange the shrimp in a single layer. Roast in the oven until just cooked through and evenly pink, about 6 minutes.

5   Arrange the shrimp on a platter, and serve with the comeback sauce, for dipping.

Note
Look for any wild-caught or untreated shrimp in packages labeled "individually frozen" in the freezer section of most good grocery stores. Oftentimes, shrimp displayed at the fish counter in grocery stores has been defrosted from frozen, so if you won't use it immediately, you might end up freezing and defrosting for a second time, which could affect the quality. Instead, opt for uncooked frozen wild-caught shrimp and defrost it yourself on an as-needed basis.

Tinned Fish Smorgasbord

Makes enough for 4 people to snack on A friend of mine and fellow tinned fish fanatic, Georgia, has a little phrase on her website that reads "If you don't like fish, try a little harder." While Georgia is pretty direct, my advice is always to try the tinned, smoked variety before giving up on fish altogether. I, too, once detested fish in a can because of the chub mackerel, mushy tuna in water, or sardines in tomato sauce of my childhood. I did, however, enjoy a smoked fish pâté from the fancy grocery store in town. It was made with snoek, a kind of smoked mackerel popular in South Africa, and there was no trace of the skin or bones, huge deterrents for me back then.

Nowadays, it's easy to find skinless, boneless varieties of high-quality fish in a can, which might nudge you to team tinned fish if you've been on the fence before. I developed a deep appreciation after discovering olive oil–packed varieties from Portugal and Spain, where preserving is an art form. Here in America, I use canned smoked kippers from Maine, which have a similar flavor profile to smoked snoek, to re-create that fancy smoked fish pâté. I serve it as part of a fun smorgasbord, with crackers and a few special tins of mackerel, sardines, and smoked mussels from the pantry. If you ever visit South Africa, take a trip to Woolworths and pick up a tub of snoek pâté to slather all over popular salted crackers known as Salticrax. Until then, serve my stateside version with your favorite crackers, pickles, and any other tinned fish you like.

SMOKED KIPPER DIP

1 (6.7-ounce) tin smoked kippers, drained

¼ cup crème fraîche (see Note)

2 tablespoons cream cheese

2 tablespoons mayonnaise

2 tablespoons fresh lemon juice

1 tablespoon chopped fresh parsley

1 tablespoon chopped fresh chives

½ teaspoon freshly ground black pepper

¼ teaspoon kosher salt

Dash of Tabasco sauce, or any vinegar-based hot sauce

FOR SERVING (OPTIONAL)

Assorted crackers (I like flatbread or sourdough crisps)

Tinned smoked mussels, sardines, or other seafood

Pickles of your choice

Seedless green grapes

1 TO MAKE THE SMOKED KIPPER DIP, in a food processor, combine the kippers, crème fraîche, cream cheese, mayonnaise, lemon juice, parsley, chives, pepper, salt, and Tabasco. Pulse until smooth and creamy, about 3 minutes. Transfer the dip to a small bowl, cover, and refrigerate for at least 30 minutes and up to 3 days before serving.

2 WHEN READY TO SERVE, place the dip on a serving board with crackers, tinned seafood, pickles, and grapes, if desired.

Note

Make your own crème fraîche by stirring together 1 cup of heavy whipping cream and 1 tablespoon of sour cream until combined. Cover and let sit at room temperature for 8 hours and up to overnight. Stir before using.

Miso Pulled Pork Nachos

Serves 4   Who doesn't love nachos? First of all, they're cheesy, and that's all the enticement that I need. Second, they're fully customizable and the perfect way to use up leftovers. In this multicultural mash-up recipe, leftover Miso-Braised Pork Shoulder (page 172) gets crisped up in a skillet with kimchi, which intensifies in flavor as it cooks. The flavorful pork is piled onto a bed of sturdy tortilla chips drenched in a quick and easy cheese sauce. Perhaps you're wondering: Why not just melt the cheese directly on the chips? Trust me, it's worth making this velvety cheese sauce. It's much more enjoyable to eat than shredded cheese, which tends to firm up and make the chips difficult to pick up, a pet peeve of mine. As for the other toppings, I once again stand by the "choose your own adventure" approach because it depends on what you have. I've suggested a few options, but at a minimum, go with pico de gallo and cilantro.

CHEESE SAUCE

1 (12-ounce) can evaporated milk

6 ounces extra-sharp Cheddar cheese, freshly shredded

1 teaspoon cornstarch

NACHOS

Half (10-ounce) bag restaurant-style tortilla chips

1 tablespoon extra-virgin olive oil

1½ cups leftover Miso-Braised Pork Shoulder (page 172), shredded

¼ cup finely chopped drained kimchi, homemade (see page 260) or store-bought

FOR SERVING (OPTIONAL)

½ cup cooked corn kernels

½ cup cooked black beans

½ cup sour cream

½ cup pico de gallo

1 large avocado, pitted and diced

Chopped fresh cilantro leaves

1   Preheat the oven to 350°F with a rack in the center position.

2   TO MAKE THE CHEESE SAUCE, in a small saucepan over medium-low heat, combine the evaporated milk, cheese, and cornstarch. Cook, stirring often, until the raw cornstarch flavor is gone and the sauce is smooth and thick enough to coat the back of a spoon, 6 to 7 minutes. Remove the saucepan from the heat, cover, and set aside. The sauce will continue to thicken as it sits. Stir before serving, and if it's too thick, reheat over low heat.

3   TO MAKE THE NACHOS, on a rimmed sheet pan, arrange the tortilla chips in a relatively even layer. Bake until heated through and crisp, 8 to 10 minutes.

4   Meanwhile, in a large skillet, heat the olive oil over medium heat. Once the oil shimmers, add the pork and kimchi, and cook, stirring occasionally, until any liquid has evaporated and the meat is crisp in places, 4 to 6 minutes.

5   ON A LARGE SERVING PLATTER (or keep them on the sheet pan for fewer dishes!), arrange the tortilla chips and drizzle evenly with ½ cup of the cheese sauce; reserve the rest of the sauce for another use (see Note). Top with the kimchi and pork, the corn, black beans, sour cream, pico de gallo, avocado, and cilantro leaves, if desired. Serve immediately.

Note

You'll have a little more of the cheese sauce than you need, but this is hardly a problem. Just refrigerate what remains in an airtight container for up to 1 week, and reheat in a small saucepan over low heat.

Grape Leaf–Grilled Camembert with Port-Simmered Raisins

Serves 2 to 4   I grew up in a place that can only be described as the African garden of Eden. This realization hit me years after leaving South Africa, when a steady, nagging voice inside started yearning for the sights and sounds of "home."

Wellington is a small town located in a lush, green valley chockablock full of vineyards, orchards, and olive groves, patchworked onto the surrounding Drakensberg mountain slopes. Most people I know work in agriculture, and in some way, everyone's life syncs up with the vines, the mist on the mountains, the dry season, and how it affects the produce or the wine.

At the end of winter pruning, farmers burn spent grapevines to prevent disease, blanketing nearby neighborhoods with a hazy smoke in the process. I always found the smell of burning grapevines to be so delectable, and this grape leaf–grilled Camembert is my rendition of that experience on a very, very, small scale.

Wrap a wheel of Camembert in brined grape leaves (available at bigger supermarkets and online), then grill the earthy cheese on the stovetop until charred. Keep the grape theme going by dressing the unwrapped cheese with warm golden raisins simmered in port. Serve the melty cheese and saucy raisins with rye or seeded Norwegian crispbread if you can—their rustic look, feel, and flavor pairs perfectly here.

6 large fresh or brined grape leaves, rinsed, patted dry, and tough stems removed

1 (8-ounce) Camembert or Brie wheel

Olive oil spray

¼ cup port, sherry, or dark rum

¼ cup golden raisins

1 tablespoon honey

1 tablespoon apple cider vinegar

½ teaspoon yellow mustard seeds

½ teaspoon freshly ground black pepper

Rye crackers or seeded Norwegian crispbread, for serving

1   Heat a grill pan or skillet over medium heat.

2   Meanwhile, on a large plate or cutting board, overlap 4 of the grape leaves, vein side up, into a 10-inch round. Place another grape leaf in the center, and put the Camembert on top. Fold the grape leaves over the Camembert to cover the cheese completely, and spray with an even coating of olive oil spray. (The olive oil spray keeps the leaves secure, but you could tie two pieces of kitchen twine around the cheese, if needed.) Transfer to the grill pan and cook, flipping halfway through, until the grape leaves are slightly charred and the cheese is melted, about 3 minutes per side. Transfer to a serving plate and let rest for 2 minutes.

3   Meanwhile, in a small skillet over medium heat, combine the port, raisins, honey, vinegar, mustard seeds, and pepper, and simmer, stirring occasionally, until the raisins are plump and the liquid is reduced by half, 1 to 2 minutes.

4   Carefully unwrap the Camembert and spoon the raisins on top. Serve with crackers.

Frozen Daiquiris

Serves 2   There's something about New Orleans that captivates everyone who visits. It's not a large city like Los Angeles or New York, it doesn't have the amenities that many other places do . . . but the culture is rich, the atmosphere soulful and proud. When I first walked down those narrow cobblestone pathways in the French Quarter, I knew that I'd keep coming back for the friendly happy-go-lucky people, delicious food, and knock-your-socks-off drinks.

If you've been to New Orleans, chances are you've had a frozen daiquiri or a frozen hurricane in one of those neon green vases they call a glass. This recipe is my re-creation of the drink in a more modest portion. You can't go wrong with the classic fruitless version, but try it with frozen peaches, mangos, strawberries, or pineapples.

½ cup light rum

¼ cup fresh lime juice

⅓ cup simple syrup (store-bought or homemade, recipe follows)

3 cups crushed ice or frozen fruit, such as sliced peaches, halved strawberries, mango, or pineapple chunks (see Note)

4 large fresh mint leaves, plus more for garnish

2 lime wedges, for garnish

In a high-speed blender, combine the rum, lime juice, simple syrup, ice or frozen fruit, and mint leaves, and blend until the drink is smooth, about 2 minutes. Divide the daiquiris between two cocktail glasses, and garnish with the lime wedges and mint leaves. Enjoy immediately.

Note
If using frozen fruit, let the fruit sit for 10 minutes at room temperature before adding to the blender. This will let it blend more easily, especially for fruit like pineapple that has a higher water content.

SIMPLE SYRUP

Makes 1 cup

1 cup sugar

1 cup water

In a small saucepan over medium heat, bring the water and sugar to a simmer, then lower the heat to low and cook, stirring occasionally, until the sugar is dissolved. Remove the saucepan from the heat, and let the syrup cool. Pour the cooled syrup into a jar, and store covered in the refrigerator for up to 1 month.

Pineapple Ginger Refresher (Pynappel Bier)

Makes 1 gallon (about 16 servings) In the summer when pineapples are abundant, set a few aside to make this South African beverage that's similar to Mexican tepache. It can be enjoyed after one day, but the fun happens on the subsequent days when the drink ferments and alcohol develops. We are okay with waiting and usually enjoy it with friends on humid 100-degree Mississippi days, served in fancy glasses with retro cocktail umbrellas. Heads-up: you'll need a large jar (that can hold more than a gallon) with a lid to make this recipe. The drink is best served chilled, preferably dressed up with pineapple wedges, cocktail cherries, and cocktail umbrellas.

1 gallon filtered water, lukewarm

1 large ripe pineapple, unpeeled, cut into 2-inch chunks

2½ cups sugar

½ cup golden raisins

1 (2-inch) piece fresh unpeeled ginger, thinly sliced

4 star anise pods

1½ teaspoons instant dry yeast

Pineapple wedges, cocktail cherries, and cocktail umbrellas, for garnish

1   In a 1½- to 2-gallon jar, combine the water with the pineapple, sugar, raisins, ginger, and star anise. Stir until the sugar is dissolved, then sprinkle in the yeast. Stir once and cover loosely with the lid.

2   Leave the pineapple refresher at room temperature for at least 24 hours, up to 2 days, stirring once or twice every day to release the gas. Taste the drink after 1 day, and if it's fermented to your liking, strain through a fine-mesh sieve into a large pitcher (you can line the sieve with cheesecloth for a perfectly clear drink), reserving the star anise pods to add back in; discard the other solids. Refrigerate for at least 2 hours before serving in glasses over ice garnished with pineapple wedges, cocktail cherries, and umbrellas.

3   The pineapple refresher can be bottled and refrigerated for up to 1 week.

Festive Season Fruit & Nuts

Makes 2½ cups   Almost everyone who grew up in Cape Town in the nineties knows the importance of having a variety of snacks in the house for the sudden uptick of visitors in December. Most families plan by squirreling away dried fruit, nuts, boxes of assorted cookies, and other nonperishable snacks for entertaining throughout the festive season. In our house, those snacks always included lightly salted mixed peanuts and raisins from Wellington Dried Fruit and Condiments Shop in town; *suur vygies*, salty-sour dried fruit of native cactus flowers purchased from the Parade (town square) in the city; and mebos, a compact chunk of dried salted apricots coated in fine sugar. These were all set out in little bowls on the formal living room table where the adults helped themselves to whatever they liked. As per my dad's rules, us kids were only allowed to dip into the supply once guests left, but it was slim pickings by then.

When I serve fruit and nuts at my informal holiday celebrations now, guests of all ages are welcome to have their fill of my favorite fruit and nut mix, a simple blend of sweet and salty maple-roasted pecans and cashews with dried cranberries and fresh, woodsy herbs.

1 cup raw pecan halves

1 cup raw cashews

2 tablespoons pure maple syrup

1 tablespoon chopped fresh herbs (I like a combination of fresh sage, rosemary, and thyme leaves)

¼ teaspoon kosher salt

½ cup dried cranberries

½ teaspoon flaky salt

1   Preheat the oven to 325°F with a rack in the center position.

2   Line a rimmed sheet pan with parchment paper. Add the pecans, cashews, maple syrup, herbs, and kosher salt, and toss together until the nuts are fully coated. Spread in an even layer, and bake until the nuts are fragrant and toasted, about 10 minutes.

3   Let the nuts cool slightly on the sheet pan, then add the cranberries and the flaky salt, and toss to combine.

4   Transfer to a serving bowl to enjoy while still warm, or let cool to room temperature and store in a sealed container in the pantry for up to 1 week.

Peachy Rooibos Iced Tea

Serves 8   On the slopes of the Cederberg mountain range in the Western Cape, the climate is temperate and the soil rich. For generations, rooibos, a broomlike fynbos plant, has grown there and enabled small farming communities to flourish. The branches are harvested with sickles in the summer and bundled by hand before undergoing an oxidation process that results in the distinctive red color and natural vanilla flavor of rooibos tea. I feel proud to serve it the way people have iced tea in the American South: steeped, sweetened, and chilled in a pitcher to sip on at a moment's notice, usually on the front porch with friends. To highlight the natural sweetness and vanilla notes of rooibos, I add a few fresh peach slices to each glass of ice before pouring the tea.

8 cups water, divided

8 bags red rooibos tea (see Note)

½ cup honey

2 large ripe peaches, pitted and cut into wedges

Lemon wedges, for garnish

1   In a medium saucepan, bring 4 cups of the water to a rolling boil over medium-high heat. Turn off the heat, add the rooibos tea bags, and steep until the liquid is dark amber in color, about 5 minutes. Remove and discard the tea bags, and stir in the honey until well combined.

2   Pour the tea into a heat-resistant pitcher, and add the remaining 4 cups of water. Refrigerate until very cold, for at least 2 hours and up to 1 week.

3   Serve the chilled tea over ice in highball glasses, with 3 to 4 peach slices per glass and a lemon wedge each, for garnish.

Note
When purchasing rooibos tea online, look for South African–owned companies to support the local communities growing this valuable export.

Watermelon & Strawberry Agua Fresca with Gochugaru Rims

Makes 2 quarts (about 6 servings)

Watermelons grown in Smith County, Mississippi, are considered to be some of the best in the country. I'm always thrilled to see pickup trucks loaded with them on the side of the main road in town, with their tattered cardboard signs that read "Smith County Watermelons! Very sweet!" displayed perfectly alongside a bright red halved watermelon to tempt passersby. I don't need any convincing. Though hauling a twenty-pound watermelon back home takes some doing, it's absolutely worth it because they are indeed bursting with flavor, and very sweet. Once we've eaten ourselves into a pulp, I make this refreshing Mexican beverage with the remaining watermelon inspired by the fruity agua fresca that we were introduced to at our first duty station in El Paso, Texas. Having grown up enjoying most fruits with a little salt and peri-peri chili for spice, I wanted to experiment a little here. Korean dried chili powder, gochugaru, has a fruity quality and great depth of flavor. Combining it with salt and sugar to embellish your highball glasses with some sweet and spicy magic before pouring the agua fresca helps to highlight the flavor of this fruity drink. If you're short on gochugaru, use any other fruity chili powder like dried ancho, pasilla, Urfa biber, or Aleppo pepper.

AGUA FRESCA

4 cups cubed seedless watermelon

1 cup sliced fresh strawberries

¼ cup sugar or honey (see Note)

¼ cup fresh lime juice (from about 3 large limes)

4 cups cold filtered water

GOCHUGARU RIM

¼ cup sugar

1 tablespoon fine gochugaru or chili powder

1 teaspoon kosher salt

1 lime wedge

4 to 6 cups ice cubes, for serving

6 lime wedges, for garnish

1   TO MAKE THE AGUA FRESCA, in a blender, combine the watermelon, strawberries, sugar, and lime juice. Blend on high power until smooth, about 1 minute. Add the water and stir.

2   TO MAKE THE GOCHUGARU RIM, on a small plate, combine the sugar, gochugaru, and salt. Run a lime wedge around each rim of six highball glasses, and then dip each rim into the prepared sugar, pressing down gently until coated.

3   Divide the ice among the rimmed glasses, and pour the agua fresca over. Garnish each drink with a fresh lime wedge, and serve immediately. Any leftover agua fresca can be stored in the refrigerator, covered, for up to 3 days.

Note

If your watermelon is particularly sweet, decrease the sugar to 2 tablespoons, and taste after blending, then stir in the remaining sugar, if desired. My husband has a sweet tooth, and we are in the South, so this amount is perfectly fine with us.

Fun Twist

I sometimes replace the watermelon and strawberries with peeled golden kiwi, pineapple, or other seasonal fruit combinations. When and if the mood strikes, replace 1 cup of water with vodka or tequila, if desired.

two

FISH
&
SHELLFISH

Cornmeal-Crusted Fish with Green Tomatoes

Serves 4   This easy weeknight dinner was inspired by fried green tomatoes, the tart, Southern cornmeal-crusted snack that I could eat by the dozen if left unsupervised. Occasionally, when luck is on my side, I answer the front door to find fishing friends who want to share their catch of trout. When somebody brings fish to your house, you'd better cook it for them! That's how I was raised, eating freshly caught seafood immediately, and always shared with the giver. In the spirit of Southern hospitality, I quickly fry up the fish for us to eat, and it goes down a treat with a dollop of Mississippi Comeback Sauce (page 59) and bright, marinated green tomatoes. The whole shebang makes for a particularly delicious dinner in the spring, but I'm also very proud to serve the meal for special occasions beyond trout season. If you're in the same boat, any firm white fish can replace trout, and sharp tomatillos are close enough in flavor to use instead of green tomatoes.

GREEN TOMATOES

2 large green tomatoes, cut into ½-inch wedges

1 green onion, chopped

2 tablespoons white wine vinegar

2 teaspoons honey

¼ teaspoon celery salt

CORNMEAL-CRUSTED FISH

½ cup buttermilk

2 teaspoons Tabasco sauce

1 cup fine cornmeal

1½ teaspoons Cajun seasoning

1 teaspoon dried parsley or dried chervil

½ cup extra-virgin olive oil

4 (6-ounce) trout, tilapia, or haddock fillets, pin bones removed

FOR SERVING (OPTIONAL)

¼ cup loosely packed torn fresh basil leaves

Mississippi Comeback Sauce (page 59)

1   TO PREPARE THE GREEN TOMATOES, in a large bowl, stir together the tomatoes, green onion, vinegar, honey, and celery salt until combined. Cover and refrigerate until ready to serve.

2   TO FRY THE FISH, in a large shallow bowl, stir together the buttermilk and Tabasco until fully combined and even in color. In another large shallow bowl, stir together the cornmeal, Cajun seasoning, and parsley. Working in batches, dip the fish fillets into the buttermilk to coat both sides, then into the cornmeal, gently pushing down to coat each side.

3   In a large skillet, heat the oil over medium-high heat until it ripples. Working in batches if necessary (you don't want the fillets touching each other in the skillet), add the fish and cook, flipping once, until light golden brown and crispy, 2 to 3 minutes per side depending on the thickness of your fish. Transfer to serving plates.

4   TO SERVE, top the fish with the green tomatoes. Sprinkle with the torn basil, and serve with the Mississippi Comeback Sauce, if desired.

Tinned Mackerel Toasts
with Anchovy Butter

Serves 2   This is my sustainable take on a tuna sandwich using canned smoked mackerel. I'm an avid collector of tinned fish from around the world and would gladly enjoy a few of them for dinner, especially in the summer when turning on an oven is the last thing on my mind. They are my go-to snack and way to serve something special to friends who stop by, without doing too much work. This toast is also a little nod to one of my favorite salads, the Niçoise, but I opt out of the typical potatoes and eggs here, and instead spoon the fish and vegetables over toasted sourdough bread spread with anchovy butter. The butter, flecked with herbs and capers, adds another layer of flavor. Swap it out for regular salted butter if you like, and feel free to replace the mackerel with any high-quality tinned fish packed in olive oil. However, do give this version a try first.

ANCHOVY BUTTER

2 tablespoons unsalted butter, softened

2 anchovy fillets, chopped

1 teaspoon stone-ground mustard

1 teaspoon finely chopped fresh parsley

1 teaspoon chopped fresh chives

½ teaspoon minced capers

MACKEREL TOASTS

1 (4- to 6-ounce) can smoked skinless mackerel fillets packed in extra-virgin olive oil

1 cup heirloom cherry tomatoes, quartered

2 ounces haricots verts, trimmed, cut into 1-inch pieces

6 pitted Kalamata olives, halved

¼ small red onion, thinly sliced

1 tablespoon fresh lemon juice or red wine vinegar

2 large slices sourdough bread, toasted

¼ teaspoon red pepper flakes (optional)

¼ cup loosely packed chopped soft fresh herbs, such as parsley, chives, and dill fronds, for serving

1   TO MAKE THE ANCHOVY BUTTER, in a small bowl, stir together the butter, anchovies, mustard, parsley, chives, and capers until well combined.

2   TO MAKE THE MACKEREL TOASTS, in a medium bowl, combine the mackerel with 1 tablespoon of the oil it's packed in, then flake into large chunks. Add the tomatoes, haricots verts, olives, onion, and lemon juice; gently toss to coat.

3   Spread the anchovy butter on the sourdough toasts. Top with the mackerel salad, then sprinkle with the red pepper flakes, if using. Garnish with the herbs and serve.

Tuesday Night
Hot-Smoked Salmon Chowder

Serves 4   Decades before marketing tactics like daily food holidays and "Taco Tuesday," my mother decided that Tuesday nights would be dedicated to cooking and eating fish. Her decision was driven by a need to "reset" after weekend cookouts and the subsequent meaty leftovers for dinner on Mondays. One of her signature dishes was neon orange smoked haddock poached in milk. As kids we were fascinated by the color and ate happily because of it. Years later in my twenties, I found out that South African "haddock" is really just Cape hake dyed with annatto, because it's cheaper to produce with the local fish. Surprisingly, the annatto never changed the color of the poaching liquid, which unfortunately my mother would discard. Looking back, I think that smoke-tinged milk must've had the most delicious flavor and could've been the creamy base for an amazing chowder, had we thought about it.

Here in America, I've been able to try a variety of sensational chowders, from New England to Seattle, and I've learned that each version is influenced by the cultures, cooking styles, and ingredients in their respective regions as well. My recipe takes inspiration from the seafood boils here in the South, with red potatoes, Creole spices, as well as onions, celery, and bell pepper (the "holy trinity" of Louisiana cuisine), all working together to deepen the flavor of the broth. The hot-smoked salmon builds on that, and as a bonus, it's orange in color just like Mom's "haddock" of yesteryear.

2 tablespoons unsalted butter

1 small yellow onion, finely chopped

½ cup finely chopped celery

¼ cup finely chopped red bell pepper

4 garlic cloves, minced

1 teaspoon Creole Seasoning (page 256) or store-bought blend

1 pound red potatoes, cut into 1-inch pieces

4 cups Chicken Stock (page 259) or store-bought low-sodium chicken broth

1 pound hot-smoked salmon (or canned or fresh smoked trout) fillet, flaked

1 cup heavy cream

Kosher salt and freshly ground black pepper

1 tablespoon chopped fresh chives, for serving

Extra-virgin olive oil, for drizzling

1   In a large Dutch oven, melt the butter over medium heat. Add the onion, celery, bell pepper, garlic, and Creole seasoning, and cook, stirring occasionally, until the onion is lightly golden and softened, 5 to 7 minutes. Add the potatoes and chicken stock, and cook, stirring occasionally, until the potatoes are fork-tender, about 15 minutes. Reduce the heat to medium-low, stir in the salmon and cream, and simmer until the flavors meld, 3 to 5 minutes. Taste and add salt and pepper if needed.

2   Ladle the chowder into bowls and sprinkle with the chives. Drizzle with olive oil and serve.

Salmon Ssam Feast

Serves 6 This gochujang-glazed salmon is a showstopper and my casual dinner party favorite because it encourages conversation and sharing! The Korean word *ssam* refers to a style of eating, where savory foods with complementary flavors are tightly bundled in lettuce or leafy vegetables and enjoyed as one harmonious bite. As a nod to the Korean custom of preparing a bite for someone you love or respect, my husband, DJ, and I take turns building each other's lettuce wraps. Some people prefer to have rice separately, but I like to include a spoonful in the ssam, along with all the tasty accompaniments. For instance, the cucumber apple salad here, while not traditional, offers a delicious freshness to go with the sweet and spicy fish—much like vegetable side dishes do in a typical Korean ssam meal. I also tuck in a little more salmon in DJ's wrap to demonstrate extra love and respect—it's great fun!

SALMON
1 (1½-pound) salmon fillet, about 1¼ inches thick

1 teaspoon kosher salt

½ teaspoon freshly ground black pepper

¼ cup Everyday Gochujang Sauce (page 259)

PICKLED CUCUMBER AND APPLE SALAD
4 Persian cucumbers, halved lengthwise and thinly sliced into half-moons

½ cup loosely packed fresh mint leaves

2 tablespoons rice wine vinegar

1 teaspoon sugar

½ teaspoon kosher salt

1 large apple

SPICY MAYONNAISE
½ cup mayonnaise

2 tablespoons Everyday Gochujang Sauce (page 259)

FOR SERVING
2 green onions, thinly sliced

1 large head butter lettuce or green leaf lettuce, leaves separated

Cooked rice (optional)

1 COOK THE SALMON: Preheat the oven to 325°F with a rack in the center position.

2 Line a rimmed sheet pan with foil, place the salmon on top, and pat dry with paper towels. Season with the salt and pepper. Using a silicone brush or the back of a spoon, spread the gochujang sauce evenly all over the top of the salmon.

3 Bake until the thickest part of the salmon reaches 135°F on an instant-read thermometer, 15 to 20 minutes. Remove from the oven and heat the broiler.

4 WHILE THE SALMON BAKES, MAKE THE SALAD: In a medium bowl, stir together the cucumber, mint, vinegar, sugar, and salt. Core, quarter, and thinly slice the apple, then stir into the bowl. Refrigerate until it's time to serve.

5 MAKE THE SPICY MAYONNAISE: In a small bowl, combine the mayonnaise with the gochujang sauce and stir to mix well.

6 FINISH THE SALMON: Broil the salmon until the glaze is sticky, about 2 minutes.

7 FOR SERVING: Transfer the salmon to a large serving platter and garnish with the green onions. Serve it alongside the spicy mayonnaise, cucumber apple salad, lettuce leaves, and individual bowls of rice, if desired.

Fish & Prosciutto Parcels
with Roasted Lemon

Serves 4   My dad had a thing for the Victoria and Alfred Waterfront in Cape Town, the oldest working harbor in the Southern Hemisphere and a popular tourist attraction located at the foot of Table Mountain. We lived about an hour away, but on Sundays, Dad would gladly make the drive. When my mom said, "Get dressed, we are going out," there was no doubt as to where we were headed, so I found the trip to be more of an obligation than an adventure. There at the harbor, seated at wooden picnic tables, we shared a "fish parcel"—battered, deep-fried hake and thick-cut potatoes drenched in malt vinegar. The name likely comes from wrapping up the fish and chips like packages in butcher paper to soak up the grease from frying. "*Konings kos!*" ("Food fit for a king!"), my dad would proclaim as he ate, teasing my sisters and me who sat there, caught up in teenage angst and embarrassment, ducking and diving as hungry seagulls swooped in to snatch our potatoes. Fun times. I dreamt of eating at fancier restaurants back then, but now, a picnic table at the harbor sounds like a dream, even if it means guarding food from hawk-eyed seagulls with thievery on their minds. It's worth it!

These are not those fish parcels, and I'm sorry to disappoint . . . but I prefer to leave deep-frying to the professionals. Hake isn't always easy to find, so any firm-fleshed fish becomes a stand-in when necessary. I do neatly package the fillets in prosciutto that crisps up in the oven, and there's your crunch factor! The meal comes together quickly on one sheet pan, and that in itself is a gift.

4 (4- to 6-ounce) skinless hake, cod, or salmon fillets

1 tablespoon stone-ground mustard

4 slices prosciutto

8 ounces sugar snap peas, strings removed, or asparagus, tough ends snapped off

1 medium lemon, thinly sliced

2 tablespoons extra-virgin olive oil

½ teaspoon kosher salt

½ teaspoon garlic powder

1 tablespoon chopped fresh parsley

1   Preheat the oven to 425°F with a rack in the center position. Line a rimmed sheet pan with parchment paper.

2   Coat the fish with the mustard, and carefully wrap each fillet with 1 slice of prosciutto.

3   On the prepared sheet pan, toss together the snap peas, lemon, olive oil, salt, and garlic powder, and arrange in a single layer. Place the prosciutto-wrapped fillets around the snap peas and lemon. Roast until the fish is cooked through, the prosciutto is crisp in places, and the snap peas are crisp-tender, 12 to 15 minutes.

4   Divide the snap peas, fish, and roasted lemon among plates. Garnish with parsley and serve.

Soul-Satisfying Fish Cake Dinner
(Eomuk Bokkeum)

Serves 4   During my very first year as an English teacher in South Korea, I was afraid to eat anything that veered too far from the familiar. It was a narrow-minded viewpoint that I deeply regret but also learned from after seeing the light. Slowly but surely my palate developed, and with it a real love for any and all Korean dishes started to blossom. The spicy, the sweet, the funky, and everything in between just grew on me, and I started to enjoy it more than the South African food of my childhood. This is one of those meals that you wouldn't know you loved until you tried it. I can't take credit for the original, a traditional Korean side dish called *eomuk bokkeum*. I learned the base recipe by watching incredible Korean American YouTubers, like Maangchi and Korean Bapsang, who generously shared their expertise online for Korean-food enthusiasts like me. Eomuk are Korean fish cakes made with pureed white fish and other ingredients such as vegetables and potato starch. You can find them in thin sheets at most Asian grocery stores either fresh or frozen. My husband and I eat the stir-fried eomuk as a main at least once a week with rice, pickled cucumbers, and a bowl of cheat's miso broth on the side. The smoky flavor of the broth with the toothsome rice, crunchy cucumber, and sweet-salty fish cakes just satisfies like nothing else. Any leftovers can be enjoyed for breakfast the next day with a sunny egg and kimchi. Don't knock it until you try it!

CHEAT'S MISO BROTH
4 cups low-sodium chicken broth

1 tablespoon white miso

2 teaspoons instant dashi powder
(Japanese bonito soup stock powder)

EASY PICKLED CUCUMBERS
2 Persian cucumbers, thinly sliced

2 teaspoons rice wine vinegar

¼ teaspoon kosher salt

STIR-FRIED FISH CAKES
2 tablespoons soy sauce

2 teaspoons sugar

1 teaspoon toasted sesame oil

1 teaspoon toasted sesame seeds

½ teaspoon freshly ground black pepper

2 tablespoons avocado or vegetable oil

4 sheets eomuk (Korean fish cakes;
8 to 10 ounces total), thawed if frozen, cut into 1-inch squares
or 1-by-2-inch rectangles

2 cups sliced cremini mushrooms

4 large garlic cloves, thinly sliced

2 green onions, cut into 1-inch pieces

1 small red bell pepper, cut into 1-inch-long strips

½ small yellow onion, cut into 1-inch pieces

¼ cup water (see Note)

1   TO MAKE THE MISO BROTH, in a medium pot over medium heat, bring the chicken broth to a simmer.

2   TO PICKLE THE CUCUMBERS, in a small bowl, combine the cucumbers, vinegar, and salt. Stir and set aside at room temperature until ready to serve.

3   In a small bowl, whisk together the miso, dashi powder, and ¼ cup of the hot chicken broth until smooth. Stir into the remaining chicken broth in the pot, and continue to simmer for 2 minutes more. Keep warm until ready to serve.

4   TO COOK THE FISH CAKES, in a small bowl, combine the soy sauce, sugar, sesame oil, sesame seeds, and black pepper; stir well and set aside.

5   In a large saucepan, heat the avocado oil over medium heat. Add the fish cakes, mushrooms, garlic, green onions, bell pepper, and onion, and cook, stirring often, until the onion is translucent and the fish cakes are lightly browned, 4 to 5 minutes. Add the water, and cover with a lid to steam until the vegetables are cooked through, 1 to 2 minutes. Add the soy sauce mixture and cook, stirring occasionally, until the fish cakes are light golden brown and the liquid is mostly evaporated, 2 to 3 to minutes more. Remove the saucepan from the heat.

6   TO SERVE, divide the miso broth among bowls. Serve with the fish cakes and pickled cucumbers.

Note

The fish cakes should double in volume once fully hydrated so adding water and letting it steam is essential, especially if your fish cakes were frozen or vacuum-sealed.

Pepper Jelly Salmon

Serves 4   This family-pleasing pepper jelly–glazed salmon is based on a popular recipe on my blog, Apricot Garlic Butter Salmon, that got a reader from Tennessee claps of approval from everyone at the dinner table. Sweet.

Traditionally, South Africans use fruit preserves and lemon on snoek, a mackerel abundant in Southern Atlantic waters. During the winter months, pickup trucks selling the fish make their way through neighborhoods in search of customers. Eager cooks wait with their Dutch doors open so they can hear the men shouting, "Snoek!" Then they rush outside to select the biggest, freshest fish before it sells out. Soon after, smoke plumes start billowing above rooftops as kindling crackles, and the fish sizzles over glowing Namibian hardwood fires.

While building a wood fire for a side of salmon is a novel way to share an integral aspect of South African culture with friends in Mississippi, it requires a bit of time and I reserve it just for special occasions. To streamline the cooking without compromising on the smokiness and stickiness that make the original dish great, I rub fillets of salmon with smoked Spanish paprika, then broil the garlicky pepper jelly glaze on top until caramelized. Any oily fish works well here: mackerel, arctic char, or steelhead trout are excellent alternatives to salmon.

1 pound salmon fillet

1 tablespoon extra-virgin olive oil

1 teaspoon kosher salt

1 teaspoon smoked paprika

3 tablespoons pepper jelly or any other fruit preserves

2 large garlic cloves, minced

1 tablespoon apple cider vinegar

2 oranges or tangerines, peeled, sliced into ¼-inch-thick rounds

¼ small red onion, thinly sliced

¼ cup pitted Castelvetrano olives, halved lengthwise

1 small serrano chili, thinly sliced (optional)

¼ cup torn fresh herbs, such as parsley, Thai basil, and mint, for garnish

1   Preheat the oven to 350°F with one rack in the center position and another rack 6 inches from the broiler.

2   Line a rimmed sheet pan with foil, place the salmon on top, and pat very dry with paper towels. Drizzle with the olive oil, then sprinkle with the salt and smoked paprika.

3   In a small bowl, stir together the pepper jelly, garlic, and vinegar until well combined. Spoon the glaze all over the top of the salmon fillet. Roast on the center oven rack until the fish flakes easily with a fork, 12 to 15 minutes. Set the oven to broil, and move the sheet pan to the upper rack. Broil, watching the salmon carefully so that it does not burn, until the glaze is slightly caramelized and sticky, 1 to 2 minutes.

4   Plate the salmon and top with the citrus slices, onion, olives, and serrano chili, if using. Garnish with the herbs and serve immediately.

Savory Sautéed Shrimp with Fresh Creamed Corn

Serves 4   Shrimp and grits are such a fixture of Southern culture that people literally judge your "Southern-ness" by the way you prepare them. Maybe that's just been my observation, but it almost leaves a transplant like me with a little trepidation. Over the years I've tried so many variations of the soulful low-country staple, from the spicy New Orleans classic, to vegetable-forward versions, and even a shrimp and grits taco—blasphemy! (jokes). There are many ways to prepare the dish, but the common goal is always one thing: flavor. I can do that.

For my summery take here, I swap out the grits for local Mississippi corn kernels, then load them up with garlic and fresh herbs. The recipe really shines during peak summer growing season, when corn is sweetest, the markets are bountiful, and the shrimp are running.

FRESH CREAMED CORN

1 tablespoon extra-virgin olive oil

½ small yellow onion, finely chopped

4 large garlic cloves, minced

4 cups fresh corn kernels

½ cup Chicken Stock (page 259) or low-sodium chicken broth

½ cup freshly grated Parmesan cheese

¼ cup heavy cream

SHRIMP

2 tablespoons extra-virgin olive oil

1 pound extra-large shrimp, peeled and deveined

1 teaspoon Greek seasoning (I like Cavender's)

1 teaspoon garlic powder

1 tablespoon fresh lemon juice

Kosher salt and freshly ground black pepper

FOR SERVING

¼ cup loosely packed roughly chopped fresh herbs, such as tarragon, chives, basil, and oregano

1   MAKE THE CORN: In a large saucepan, heat the olive oil over medium heat. Add the onion and garlic, and cook, stirring occasionally, until the onion is translucent and the garlic is fragrant, 2 to 3 minutes. Add the corn and chicken stock, and cook, covered, until the corn is tender and the stock is reduced by half, 5 to 6 minutes. Reduce the heat to low, then add the Parmesan and heavy cream, stirring until the cheese is melted and the sauce is slightly thickened. Cover and set aside.

2   COOK THE SHRIMP: In a large skillet, heat the olive oil over medium heat. Meanwhile, in a large bowl, combine the shrimp, Greek seasoning, and garlic powder, and toss until the shrimp is fully coated. Once the oil is hot, add the shrimp and cook, stirring occasionally, until the shrimp just turns pink and is no longer opaque, 1 to 2 minutes. Stir in the lemon juice. Taste and add salt and pepper, if needed. Remove the skillet from the heat.

3   FOR SERVING: Divide the corn among four bowls, and spoon a generous amount of the shrimp on top, then sprinkle with the herbs.

Pasta with Scallops & Lemony Garlic Butter

Serves 2 to 4   If you find yourself feeling a little daunted about cooking scallops, just remember to buy firm, fresh scallops and pat them very dry before cooking. As they finish cooking, I like to baste them with my flavorful Preserved Lemon Garlic Butter, which combines with white wine to form the sauce for the pasta tossed in the skillet.

Kosher salt

8 ounces fettuccine or linguine

1 pound large diver scallops, patted dry with paper towels (see Note)

1 tablespoon extra-virgin olive oil

4 tablespoons Preserved Lemon Garlic Butter (recipe follows)

¼ cup dry white wine, such as Chardonnay

1 cup cherry tomatoes

1 cup fresh corn kernels

1 small zucchini, halved lengthwise (quartered, if large) and sliced crosswise ¼ inch thick

¼ cup roughly chopped fresh herbs, such as chives or basil, oregano, and parsley, for garnish

1   Bring a large pot of salted water to a rolling boil. Add the pasta and cook according to the package instructions.

2   Season the scallops on each side with ½ teaspoon salt. In a large skillet, heat the olive oil over medium-high heat until just smoking. Add the scallops and cook, undisturbed, until golden brown on the bottom, 1½ to 2 minutes. Flip and add the preserved lemon garlic butter, then continue to cook, spooning the melted butter over the scallops, until the sides are firm, 1 to 1½ minutes. Transfer the scallops to a plate and tent with foil to keep warm. Reduce the heat to medium. Add the wine to the skillet and cook, scraping any browned bits off the bottom of the skillet with a wooden spoon, until reduced by half, about 1 minute. Add the tomatoes, corn, and zucchini, and cook, stirring occasionally, until some tomatoes start to burst and the zucchini is just cooked, about 3 minutes. Taste and add more salt, if needed.

3   Drain the pasta, then add to the skillet and toss until combined.

4   Divide the pasta among plates, top with the scallops, and garnish with the herbs. Serve immediately.

Note

You can substitute the scallops with (4-ounce, ½-inch-thick) ahi tuna steaks or salmon fillets, or 1 pound of large shrimp. Cook them for 1½ to 2 minutes on each side, more if your fish or shrimp is thicker or larger.

PRESERVED LEMON GARLIC BUTTER

Makes ½ cup

Lemon rind, while bitter when fresh, mellows out after being preserved, and that's why it's a wonderful ingredient in the kitchen. Adding preserved lemon rind to everyday recipes like this garlic butter is a fun and unexpected way to boost the flavor of pasta, any seafood dish, roasted chicken, and garlic bread.

1 stick (8 tablespoons) salted butter, softened

1 tablespoon minced rind from Preserved Lemons (page 258) or the zest of 2 large lemons

1 tablespoon finely chopped fresh parsley

4 large garlic cloves, minced

In a small bowl, combine the butter, preserved lemon rind, parsley, and garlic. Mix until evenly incorporated.

Shrimp Tacos
with Peri-Peri Yogurt Sauce

Serves 4 (8 tacos) I never subscribed to the Taco Tuesday movement because any day is a good day for tacos, don't you agree? Especially shrimp tacos because they cook up in a flash. For a little extra heat, I add a few tablespoons of my Garlic Peri-Peri Sauce to the creamy yogurt sauce drizzled over the tacos. I serve them family-style as a way to keep dinner conflict-free, due to a silly debate I have with my husband regarding how to build the perfect taco. He likes his shrimp at the bottom of the tortilla and slaw on top to prevent any of the precious seafood from falling out (it low-key does make sense). I prefer the shrimp on top for the aesthetics. However you build the tacos, they're a surefire way to satisfy your cravings, any day. You may have some extra limes on hand when making these, so some Frozen Daiquiris (page 65) couldn't hurt either.

SHRIMP
24 extra-large peeled, deveined shrimp (about 1 pound)

Grated zest and juice of 1 small lime

1 teaspoon chipotle chili powder

1 teaspoon garlic powder

½ teaspoon kosher salt

2 tablespoons avocado oil

PERI-PERI YOGURT SAUCE
½ cup Greek yogurt or sour cream

¼ cup mayonnaise

2 tablespoons Garlic Peri-Peri Sauce (page 262) or your favorite hot sauce

1 tablespoon honey

¼ teaspoon garlic powder

¼ teaspoon kosher salt

SLAW
1 jicama, peeled and julienned (about 2 cups)

1 cup shredded cabbage or prepackaged coleslaw mix

¼ small red onion, thinly sliced

¼ cup loosely packed cilantro leaves

2 tablespoons fresh lime juice

¼ teaspoon kosher salt

FOR SERVING
8 corn tortillas, warmed

1 small jalapeño or serrano chili, thinly sliced (optional)

1 MARINATE THE SHRIMP: In a large bowl, combine the shrimp, lime zest, lime juice, chipotle chili powder, garlic powder, and salt. Toss to coat and set aside to marinate at room temperature for 15 minutes.

2 MEANWHILE, MAKE THE PERI-PERI YOGURT SAUCE: In a small serving bowl, combine the yogurt, mayonnaise, garlic peri-peri sauce, honey, garlic powder, and salt, and whisk together until well combined.

3 MAKE THE SLAW: In a large serving bowl, toss together the jicama, cabbage, red onion, cilantro, lime juice, and salt until well combined.

4 COOK THE SHRIMP: In a large skillet, heat the avocado oil over medium-high heat. Once the oil shimmers, add the shrimp and cook, stirring occasionally, until pink all over and fully cooked through, about 3 minutes.

5 To assemble the tacos my way, place some of the slaw on each tortilla, and top each one with 3 shrimp. Drizzle with the yogurt sauce, and top with the sliced chili, if using. Alternatively, put everything on the table with utensils and serve, family-style.

West Coast Mussels

Serves 4   There's a restaurant on the beach in the town of Langebaan on the west coast of South Africa called The Strandloper, where locals cook whole fish, halved rock lobster with garlic butter, and mussels in white wine over live fires for hungry tourists willing to pay top dollar for that experience. To the side of the fires, fresh loaves of bread bake in wood-fired clay ovens to be served tableside, spread thick with farm butter and apricot jam—a classic South African accompaniment to seafood.

In my family, rock lobster was reserved for special occasions like Christmas, and even then, adults had first dibs, leaving us kids with a meager taste. Mussels, on the other hand, have always been abundant in coastal South Africa and could be harvested for free from the moss-covered rocks that lined the shore. Their shells will probably always wash up on the beaches in Langebaan, crunching underneath feet walking toward the milky blue-green water. I spent a lot of time on those idyllic beaches, collecting the shiniest shells with my sisters in the sun while my uncle fished, then returning home to eat mussels with sandwich bread, apricot jam, and margarine. Here at home in Mississippi, I re-create that meal with the occasional pot of mussels, some great bread, grass-fed butter, and the best apricot jam or preserves that I can find. Turns out, rock lobster isn't my thing, after all.

1 tablespoon extra-virgin olive oil

4 strips thick-cut uncured bacon (about 4 ounces), finely chopped

2 large shallots, finely diced

1 small fresh Fresno chili, thinly sliced

8 garlic cloves, minced

½ teaspoon ground coriander

½ cup dry white wine

2 tablespoons fresh lemon juice

2 pounds fresh mussels, scrubbed and debearded, if necessary (see Note)

1 cup heavy cream

2 tablespoons chopped fresh parsley

FOR SERVING

Crusty sourdough bread

Salted grass-fed butter

Best-quality apricot jam or preserves (this is VERY optional)

Lemon wedges (optional)

1   In a large pot with a glass lid, or large Dutch, heat the oil oven over medium heat. (If you have a large shallow braiser with a glass lid, even better. You'll be able to see the mussels open without having to lift the lid, which would let the steam escape.) Add the bacon, shallots, chili, garlic, and coriander, and cook, stirring occasionally, until the shallots are soft and the bacon is cooked, 5 to 6 minutes. Add the wine and lemon juice, and bring to a boil over medium-high heat. Tip in the mussels and cook, covered, until the mussels open, 5 to 6 minutes. Remove the pot from the heat and discard any unopened mussels. Stir in the heavy cream and sprinkle everything with the parsley.

2   Ladle the mussels and broth into a large serving bowl. Serve with bread, butter, apricot jam, and lemon wedges, if desired.

Note

Most mussels available for purchase today are farm-raised and require less cleaning than the ones I grew up with. I still double check that they are clean by placing them in a large bucket of salted cold water for a few hours so that they can purge any grit or sand before cooking. Discard any that are open before you start, as those have died.

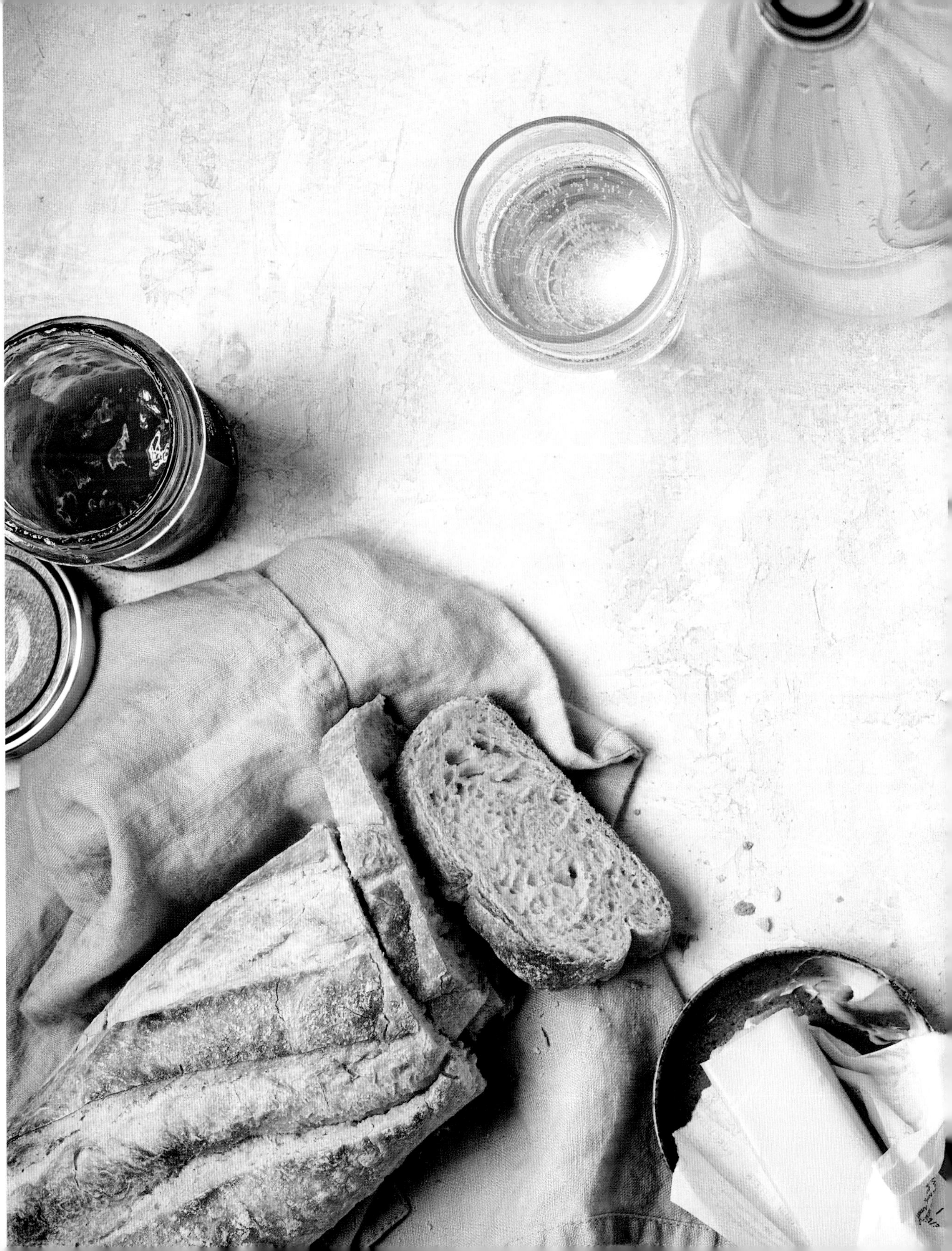

WEST COAST MUSSELS, 95

Shrimp Fried Rice, Cape Town Style

Serves 4   Year-round, my youngest sister, Kim, and I reminisce about the shrimp with fragrant yellow rice at one of our favorite restaurants at the Victoria and Alfred Waterfront in Cape Town. Usually we do this over a video call, with one of us in the depths of winter and the other experiencing the height of summer, thanks to living in different hemispheres. Talk of freshly caught, flavorful seafood in Cape Town keeps us going. During my trips back to South Africa, Kim and I always make a point of celebrating my return with a seafood feast just between us two sisters.

Here at home in Mississippi, I take full advantage of the abundance of Gulf shrimp. It's my interpretation of that Cape Town shrimp and rice platter, but stir-fried all together in a skillet!

1 pound large shrimp, peeled and deveined (see Note)

1 teaspoon kosher salt

¼ teaspoon freshly cracked black pepper

2 tablespoons extra-virgin olive oil

½ small yellow onion, finely chopped

¼ small red bell pepper, finely diced

4 garlic cloves, minced

1 teaspoon peeled and minced fresh ginger

1½ teaspoons ground coriander

½ teaspoon ground cumin

¼ teaspoon ground turmeric

2 tablespoons fresh lemon juice

4 cups day-old cooked rice, crumbled by hand to separate the grains

2 tablespoons chopped fresh cilantro leaves, plus ½ cup loosely packed cilantro leaves for serving

1   In a large bowl, season the shrimp with the salt and pepper, and toss to coat.

2   In a large skillet, heat the oil over medium heat. Add the shrimp and cook, stirring often, until just cooked through and pink, about 3 minutes. Using a slotted spoon, transfer the shrimp to a plate.

3   To the same skillet, add the onion, bell pepper, garlic, ginger, coriander, cumin, and turmeric, and cook over medium heat, stirring occasionally, until the onion just starts to soften and the spices are fragrant, 3 to 5 minutes. Add the lemon juice, and scrape any browned bits and spices from the bottom of the skillet with a wooden spoon. Add the rice and cook, stirring occasionally, until uniformly yellow and heated through, 3 to 5 minutes. Stir in the shrimp and chopped cilantro, and sprinkle with the whole cilantro leaves before serving.

Note

The shrimp can be swapped out for 1 pound of calamari rings, precooked mussels on the half shell, or firm white fish cut into 1-inch pieces.

Crab Cakes Piccata

Serves 4   This recipe was inspired by my favorite crab cake at Char, a restaurant in Jackson, Mississippi, where they serve it with a rich butter sauce. For my homespun interpretation, lemon juice, parsley, and capers are stirred into the sauce in the style of Italian American piccata. They add a welcome brightness to the crab cake as well as any vegetables served alongside, making them instantly more delicious—it's especially good on haricots verts. Even so, I'm well aware that good crab cakes are perfect as is, and adding a buttery sauce might be gilding the lily here, so feel free to skip the piccata sauce if you prefer to keep it simple. In that case, serve the crab cakes with lemon wedges, for squeezing.

CRAB CAKES

2 large eggs

2 tablespoons mayonnaise

1 green onion, finely chopped

1 tablespoon Dijon mustard

2 teaspoons Worcestershire sauce

2 large garlic cloves, minced

1 teaspoon Cajun seasoning, or Old Bay

1 pound cooked lump crab claw meat, picked through
for any shells

⅓ cup panko bread crumbs

1 tablespoon extra-virgin olive oil

PICCATA SAUCE

4 tablespoons unsalted butter

2 garlic cloves, minced

1 cup Chicken Stock (page 259) or store-bought low-sodium
chicken stock

1 tablespoon fresh lemon juice

1 tablespoon finely chopped fresh parsley

1 tablespoon capers

1   TO MAKE THE CRAB CAKES, in a large bowl, whisk together the eggs, mayonnaise, green onion, mustard, Worcestershire sauce, garlic, and Cajun seasoning until well combined. Add the crabmeat and bread crumbs, and stir gently until well incorporated. Divide into 4 patties, packing each into a ½-cup measuring cup and letting the excess come over the rim of the cup, then tip out onto a sheet pan. Gently flatten the crab cakes into 1-inch-thick rounds. Cover and refrigerate for 30 minutes to 1 hour so they can firm up and stay intact in the skillet.

2   In a large skillet, heat the oil over medium heat. Once the oil shimmers, add the crab cakes and cook until golden brown, 3 to 5 minutes per side. Transfer to a plate.

3   TO MAKE THE SAUCE, in the same skillet over medium heat, melt the butter. Add the garlic and cook, stirring often, until fragrant but not browned, about 15 seconds. Add the chicken stock and cook until reduced by half, 5 to 6 minutes.

4   Reduce the heat to medium-low, then stir in the lemon juice, parsley, and capers. Return the crab cakes to the skillet to heat through, spoon over some of the sauce in the skillet, and serve.

three

POULTRY

Marry Me Chicken Soup

Serves 8   In our house, *dakdoritang*, a hearty Korean chicken stew with potatoes and carrots, is sentimentally referred to as "marry me chicken" because it was simmering away on the stovetop the night that DJ proposed. We were in Korea at the time, and I was frustrated because of a mishap at work. I started dinner by cooking rather aggressively, butchering the whole chicken with a cleaver while tears ran down my face. I must've zoned out for a while judging from the smell of burnt onions in the air, but when I turned around to kill the heat he was kneeling with a ring. Perfect timing. What mishap at work? What burnt onions? We ate as an engaged couple for the first time that night, all that happiness leading to calmer cooking, and a sense of optimism. I've since made it a rule never to cook when upset, remembering my mother's maxim: "The mood of the cook affects the food."

I've been blissfully serving up this chicken soup inspired by dakdoritang since then, opting for the convenience of an Instant Pot. My recipe is extra brothy and milder than dakdoritang, with a hit of rice wine vinegar for more tang. When I want extra richness, I dollop the soup with sour cream, which gets livened up with a flurry of perilla and chili slices. Perilla is a fragrant anise-scented Korean herb that I grow in the yard specifically for my favorite Korean recipes. They aren't traditional in dakdoritang, but the flavor adds a lot of brightness to the soup. Most larger Korean grocery stores like H Mart stock them in the produce section, but if you cannot find perilla leaves, just omit them and add a sprinkle of green onions to each bowl right before serving.

1 large yellow onion, chopped

4 green onions, chopped (see Note)

1 small fresh Fresno chili or jalapeño, seeded and chopped

1 tablespoon toasted sesame oil

1 teaspoon kosher salt, plus more to taste

6 large garlic cloves, minced

2-inch piece fresh ginger, peeled and minced

1½ pounds bone-in chicken thighs, skin removed, trimmed of excess fat

4 cups roughly chopped green cabbage (about ¼ medium cabbage)

4 medium potatoes or sweet potatoes (I like Japanese sweet potatoes), peeled, if desired, and cut into 1-inch chunks

2 large carrots, peeled and cut into 1-inch chunks

1 tablespoon mild gochujang

6 cups Chicken Stock (page 259) or low-sodium chicken broth

2 tablespoons rice wine vinegar or lemon juice

FOR SERVING (OPTIONAL)

½ cup sour cream

2 to 4 Korean perilla leaves, tough stems removed, roughly chopped

1 small fresh Fresno chili or jalapeño, thinly sliced

Toasted sesame seeds

continues on page 106

1   Set an Instant Pot or other multicooker to sauté on medium heat (or set a large Dutch oven over medium heat). Add the onion, green onions, chili, sesame oil, and salt, and cook, stirring occasionally, until the onion is translucent and light golden brown, 3 to 4 minutes.

2   Add the garlic and ginger, and cook, stirring occasionally, until fragrant, about 2 minutes more. Add the chicken, cabbage, potatoes, carrots, and gochujang, and stir together until coated. Pour in the chicken stock. Lock the lid and set to pressure-cook on medium for 10 minutes. (Or cover the Dutch oven and bring to a boil over high heat, then lower the heat to medium, and cook, covered, until the chicken is cooked through and the vegetables are very tender, 20 to 25 minutes.)

3   Let the steam do a natural release from the Instant Pot for 15 minutes, then switch to the venting position to release the remaining steam. Using tongs, remove the chicken bones and any cartilage in the soup, and discard. Stir in the vinegar.

4   Divide the soup among bowls, and top each with a dollop of the sour cream, the perilla leaves, chili slices, and a sprinkling of toasted sesame seeds, if desired.

Note

A lady at H Mart once told me that she simmers the green onion roots for soup broth, because they contain a lot of flavor. I recommend doing so here—just rub away any dirt from the roots under running water and add them along with the rest of the green onions. If you're in the heart of leek season, ½ cup of finely chopped leeks are a good substitute for green onions.

Smoky Chicken-Topped Sweet Potatoes

Serves 4   These roasted sweet potatoes are topped with smoky chicken and vegetables, and I reach for them often when craving an easy, balanced, all-in-one kind of dinner. Chipotles in adobo add the smokiness and a little heat that's mellowed out with creamy coconut milk.

To save time, I make the dish with chicken that's already cooked (having leftover roasted chicken or Costco rotisserie on hand is a weeknight lifesaver). The recipe is a great vehicle for any cooked proteins, grains, or greens in the refrigerator, so customize the sweet potato with what you have. Try broccolini or spinach instead of kale, and cooked lentils or black beans could easily stand in for the chicken. Do try to add the pickled onions, though. They balance out the rich sweet potatoes with a nice sharpness.

2 large sweet potatoes, scrubbed (see Note)

2 tablespoons extra-virgin olive oil, divided

8 cups chopped kale (stems and tough ribs removed)

1 small yellow onion, finely chopped

½ small red bell pepper, finely chopped

4 large garlic cloves, minced

1 or 2 chipotle chilis in adobo, finely chopped

2 tablespoons tomato paste

2 teaspoons chopped fresh oregano leaves,
plus more for garnish (optional)

1 teaspoon kosher salt

1 teaspoon smoked paprika

1 teaspoon garlic powder

¼ teaspoon ground cumin

½ cup Chicken Stock (page 259) or low-sodium chicken broth

¼ cup coconut milk

1 pound shredded cooked chicken

½ cup Easy Pickled Red Onions (page 107),
drained, for serving

1   Preheat the oven to 425°F with a rack in the center position.

2   Place the sweet potatoes on a rimmed sheet pan and roast until fork-tender, 35 to 40 minutes.

3   Meanwhile, in a large saucepan, heat 1 tablespoon of the olive oil over medium heat. When the oil shimmers, add the kale and cook, stirring often, until bright green and wilted, about 1 minute. Transfer to a plate. To the skillet, add the remaining 1 tablespoon olive oil, the onion, and bell pepper, and cook, stirring occasionally, until the onion just starts to soften, 3 to 5 minutes. Add the garlic and cook, stirring, until fragrant, about 30 seconds. Add the chipotles, tomato paste, oregano, salt, smoked paprika, garlic powder, and cumin, and cook, stirring occasionally, until the spices are fragrant, 1 to 2 minutes. Stir in the chicken stock, coconut milk, and chicken, and cook, uncovered, until the sauce has thickened slightly and the flavors meld, about 5 minutes.

4   Cut the sweet potatoes in half lengthwise. Place each half on a dinner plate, then top with the kale, chicken mixture and sauce, and pickled onions, dividing evenly. Garnish with oregano leaves, if desired, and serve.

Note
In a rush? No worries! Bake a bag of frozen sweet potato fries in the oven, or slice your sweet potatoes into wedges and drizzle with olive oil to roast them in half the time.

Lifesaving Lemon Pepper Chicken Patties

Serves 6   I always thought I'd be a mom one day.

A few months before first meeting my now husband, DJ, a girl's name came to mind and stuck. Ruby. I thought it was perfect because though I didn't personally know anyone named Ruby, all the Rubys on television seemed to have a lot of sass. For years I dreamt of my daughter, Ruby, who had curly hair like me and was confident, outspoken, and funny. One of the first conversations that I had with DJ was about how many kids we would have. Newly in love, lofty future plans dripped from our lips like honey. We pondered potential names for a daughter. He heard my response and paused. "Ruby."

Ruby was his grandmother's name, you see. She had passed away a few months prior, and though I never got a chance to meet her, everyone describes her as funny, outspoken, and a little bit sassy. The photos in DJ's childhood home show a curly haired woman with kind eyes hugging her grandchildren. It must have been meant to be.

We got married and started trying, but year after year rolled by without any luck. Ruby. The idea of her became my lighthouse when one round of IVF after the other left us drained. On nights when cooking felt burdensome my dinner goal was just to get food on the table quickly. We still had each other, and we still needed to eat.

Ground chicken became a lifesaver because it cooked up fast. When turning them into patties, I also discovered that running out of eggs (pun not intended) was no big deal because a little extra sour cream did wonders to keep the chicken juicy.

These patties remain a dinner staple as we continue in search of our beacon, Ruby, and I share it with anyone going through the tides of life.

1 pound ground chicken (85% lean/15% fat ratio, for best results)

4 garlic cloves, minced

2 tablespoons finely chopped fresh parsley

3 tablespoons sour cream

1 medium lemon, zested (1 teaspoon) and cut into wedges for serving

2 teaspoons lemon pepper seasoning

½ teaspoon kosher salt

⅛ teaspoon cayenne pepper

2 tablespoons extra-virgin olive oil

Yogurt Feta Sauce (page 263; optional)

1   In a large bowl, combine the chicken, garlic, parsley, sour cream, lemon zest, lemon pepper seasoning, salt, and cayenne. Gently stir with a fork until the mixture comes together and the seasoning is evenly distributed.

2   In a large skillet, heat the oil over medium heat. When the oil shimmers, swirl the skillet to completely coat the bottom with oil. Meanwhile, divide the chicken into six portions and flatten each into a 1-inch-thick patty, gently placing in the skillet as soon as you form it. (The patties may look wet at this point but they will come together in the skillet.) Cook, briefly reshaping the patties with a spatula if needed, until golden brown, 3 to 4 minutes on each side.

3   Transfer the patties to plates. Serve with the feta sauce, if desired, and the lemon wedges. Refrigerate any leftovers in an airtight container for up to 3 days.

Skillet Jezebel Chicken with Peach & Herb Salad

Serves 4   This is a sweet and salty combination inspired by one of my favorite Southern recipes, Jezebel sauce. Typically made with pineapple preserves and mustard, Jezebel sauce is served as a dip or a condiment with proteins like roast pork. Using preserves in everyday cooking is right up my alley as most older South African recipes contain some sort of preserve, a reminder of a time when my ancestors fused local Cape fruit with more assertive spices from Malaysia and Indonesia to form what is today known as Cape Malay cuisine. Here, I toss chicken thighs in peach preserves, whole-grain mustard, and white balsamic vinegar, then cook them quickly in a skillet. The umami-laden chicken is served alongside a simple salad with marinated feta, grilled peaches, and fresh herbs—a meal that just begs to be eaten on a balmy summer's day.

CHICKEN

3 tablespoons white balsamic vinegar

2 tablespoons whole-grain mustard

1 tablespoon peach preserves or honey

2 teaspoons kosher salt

1 teaspoon freshly ground black pepper

1 teaspoon chopped fresh thyme leaves

1 teaspoon paprika

1 teaspoon garlic powder

1½ pounds boneless skinless chicken thighs, excess fat trimmed

1 tablespoon extra-virgin olive oil

SALAD

4 ounces feta cheese, cut into chunks

2 tablespoons white balsamic vinegar

1 teaspoon crushed pink peppercorns

3½ tablespoons extra-virgin olive oil, divided

2 medium peaches, pitted and cut into ½-inch wedges

4 cups tender lettuce leaves or baby greens

¼ red onion, thinly sliced

½ cup loosely packed fresh tender herbs, such as dill fronds or tarragon and mint leaves, for serving

1   TO COOK THE CHICKEN, in a large bowl, combine the vinegar, mustard, peach preserves, salt, pepper, thyme, paprika, and garlic powder, and stir until well blended. Add the chicken and toss until well coated.

2   In a large nonstick skillet, heat the olive oil over medium heat. Swirl the skillet to coat the bottom with oil, then add the chicken and cook, flipping halfway through and lowering the heat if the marinade threatens to burn, until deep golden brown and cooked through, 4 to 5 minutes per side. Transfer to a large serving platter.

3   MEANWHILE, MAKE THE SALAD. In a small, shallow bowl, add the feta, top with the vinegar, pink peppercorns, and 3 tablespoons of the olive oil.

4   Heat a grill pan over medium heat. Meanwhile, in a medium bowl, toss together the peaches and remaining ½ tablespoon olive oil until well coated. Grill the peaches until slightly charred, about 1 minute per side.

5   Arrange the lettuce, grilled peaches, onion, and marinated feta alongside the chicken. Drizzle the salad with a few tablespoons of the feta marinade, then scatter with the herbs.

Chicken & Mushroom Phyllo Pie (Hoenderpastei)

Serves 4 to 6   If you're expecting a classic American chicken pot pie with peas and carrots, then perhaps you'll be disappointed, or maybe this easy take on my mother's chicken pie will delight you! Mom still flavors her filling with canned mushroom soup and slowly simmers a young chicken with warm spices like cloves, then meticulously separates meat from bone. The cooled filling is sandwiched between two layers of rolled-out puff pastry, then baked until golden. Meanwhile, with a floury handprint on her apron, Mom wipes the countertops and hand-washes the pots. Her chicken pie is a dream to eat, but a nightmare when it comes to cleanup.

Mom's pie is based on a Dutch recipe first introduced to South Africa as far back as 1669 so perhaps it's no surprise that it takes a few hours to prepare. Sorry, Mom, but I had to give it a less time-consuming refresh. Instead of using a whole chicken and mushroom soup, I like a fifty-fifty blend of ground chicken and button mushrooms. I flavor the filling with poultry seasoning because it contains all the herbs without having to wash and chop fresh ones, plus a smidgen of ground cloves for that nostalgic taste of home. Phyllo sheets are a simpler replacement for the puff pastry because they don't require rolling out or any flour to scrape from the counter, plus they're perfectly crispy and beautifully golden once baked. Given how much quicker this version is, I think Mom will forgive the liberties I've taken.

FILLING

1 tablespoon extra-virgin olive oil

1 medium yellow onion, finely chopped

1 pound ground chicken thighs

1 pound button mushrooms, sliced

4 large garlic cloves, minced

1 teaspoon kosher salt

1 teaspoon coarsely ground black pepper

1 teaspoon poultry seasoning

1 teaspoon porcini powder (optional)

¼ teaspoon ground cloves

½ cup dry white wine, such as Sauvignon Blanc or Chardonnay

2 tablespoons cornstarch

1 cup Chicken Stock (page 259) or low-sodium chicken broth

2 tablespoons fresh lemon juice

2 tablespoons heavy whipping cream (optional)

Flaky salt, for serving

Fresh thyme leaves, for serving

ASSEMBLY

Extra-virgin olive oil spray

Twelve 13 × 18-inch sheets phyllo pastry (see Note)

continues

1 TO MAKE THE FILLING, in a large Dutch oven, heat the oil oven over medium heat. Add the onion and cook, stirring occasionally, until light golden brown, 4 to 5 minutes. Add the chicken, mushrooms, garlic, salt, pepper, poultry seasoning, porcini powder, if using, and cloves, and cook, stirring occasionally and breaking up any lumps of chicken with a wooden spoon, until the chicken is no longer pink and the mushrooms are softened, 4 to 5 minutes. Pour in the wine and cook, scraping any browned bits off the bottom of the pot with the wooden spoon, until the wine is reduced by half, about 2 minutes. Stir in the cornstarch, then pour in the chicken stock and cook, stirring occasionally, until the liquid is thickened and reduced by half, 5 to 6 minutes. Stir in the lemon juice and heavy cream, if using. Let cool to room temperature if filling the pie right away, or chill in the refrigerator for up to 2 days if filling the pie later.

2 TO ASSEMBLE THE PIE, preheat the oven to 375°F with a rack in the center position. Spray the bottom and sides of an 8-inch pie dish with olive oil spray.

3 Stack the phyllo sheets and cover with a damp kitchen towel. Working swiftly with one sheet at a time, line the bottom of the pie dish, letting the phyllo hang over the sides; lightly coat the entire sheet with olive oil spray. Continue lining the pan, turning the pan clockwise and spraying each sheet, until only 4 sheets remain.

4 Spoon the cooled pie filling into the pan in an even layer. Cover the top with the remaining 4 phyllo sheets, again spraying, turning, and letting the phyllo hang over the sides. Fold the overhanging pastry onto the top and give it one last spray. Bake until the pastry is golden brown and evenly crisp, 40 to 45 minutes.

5 Carefully invert the pie onto a large serving plate, then sprinkle with flaky salt and thyme leaves and cut into wedges.

Note

Phyllo has a tendency to dry out quickly when exposed to air, so prepare all the other ingredients before taking it out of its packaging to prevent this from happening. Cover the unrolled pastry with a clean damp kitchen towel or paper towel as you layer and work gently to avoid ripping.

Chicken with Chorizo & Olives, by Request

Serves 4 This recipe is a favorite of blog readers, who insisted that I add it to the book for their reference. Here you have it, friends! I can see the appeal: It's moreish and combines pantry staples like canned tomatoes, jarred olives, and herbs with chicken thighs that braise in the oven, yet has enough pizzazz to impress even the most discerning guests for special dinners. Serve this simple chicken and olive dish with lots of crusty bread, or over polenta or pasta to soak up every bit of the flavorful sauce.

4 bone-in skin-on chicken thighs (1½ to 2 pounds; see Notes)

1 teaspoon kosher salt

1 teaspoon freshly cracked black pepper

1 teaspoon smoked paprika

2 tablespoons extra-virgin olive oil

2 fresh rosemary sprigs, needles stripped

1 medium yellow onion, chopped

6 garlic cloves, minced

4 ounces Spanish chorizo, sliced ¼ inch thick (see Notes)

1 tablespoon red wine vinegar

1 (14.5-ounce) can whole San Marzano tomatoes, crushed by hand

1½ cups Chicken Stock (page 259) or low-sodium chicken broth

1 cup mixed olives, pitted (see Notes)

¼ cup chopped roasted red peppers

1 pint cherry tomatoes on the vine

2 tablespoons fresh lemon juice, for serving (optional)

1 On a large plate, season the chicken with the salt, pepper, and smoked paprika. Let sit, covered, at room temperature for 30 minutes, or refrigerated up to overnight for best results. If refrigerating, remove the chicken 1 hour before cooking.

2 Preheat the oven to 375°F with a rack in the center position.

3 In a large oven-safe skillet or braiser, heat the oil over medium heat. Add the rosemary needles and cook, stirring, until the oil no longer sizzles and the leaves are crispy, 15 to 30 seconds. Using a slotted spoon, transfer the rosemary to a plate and set aside, reserving the oil in the skillet.

4 To the reserved oil, add the chicken, skin side down, and cook over medium heat until golden brown and crisp, 3 to 4 minutes per side. Transfer the chicken to a plate.

5 To the same skillet, add the onion, garlic, and chorizo, and cook over medium heat, stirring occasionally, until the fat is rendered from the chorizo, coating the onion, and the garlic is fragrant, 3 to 5 minutes. Add the vinegar and cook, until evaporated, scraping any browned bits off the bottom of the skillet with a wooden spoon. Add the canned tomatoes, chicken stock, olives, and red peppers, and cook, stirring occasionally, until the liquid is slightly reduced, about 5 minutes. Transfer the chicken, skin side up, back to the skillet, nestling it into the sauce. Arrange the vines of cherry tomatoes on top and transfer to the oven.

6 Roast until the thickest part of the thighs near the bone reaches 165°F on an instant-read thermometer, 25 to 30 minutes.

7 Drizzle the chicken with the lemon juice, if using, then sprinkle with the reserved crispy rosemary.

continues

Notes

If using chicken breasts, I highly recommend skin on. The cooking time will vary based on the thickness of your chicken, but I keep an instant-read thermometer close by so that I can pull it from the oven at 165°F. Insert the thermometer into the thickest part of the breast to determine doneness.

You'll need Spanish chorizo (the firm kind, not Mexican chorizo) for this recipe, but if that is unavailable, add 1 teaspoon each of smoked paprika and oregano when simmering the sauce.

When it comes to olives, the easiest way to buy a selection is the olive bar at your local grocery store, but any kind will do. Castelvetrano olives, a buttery green Italian variety with a meaty texture, are an excellent choice as most of the olive-hating people in my life seem to love their milder taste. If your olives come packed in oil, you can use that oil to sear the chicken, provided there is no water mixed in. This will boost that olive flavor even more.

Garlic & Herb Chicken Flattie

Serves 2 to 4   This is my version of my mom's juicy, crispy-skinned everyday chicken that was so good, it made anyone waiting for dinner want to snatch a piece right off the sheet pan as it emerged from the hot oven. Mom seasoned chicken pieces generously with ready-made dry rubs, then broiled the seasoned chicken on the center rack instead of roasting, which helped it cook up in record time, and gave it the crackling skin that we so loved. I prefer this technique to roasting and use it for this garlic and herb butter–basted chicken when those cravings for classic home-cooked meals hit.

Because this chicken is spatchcocked, it cooks evenly in under an hour, making it a very doable last-minute dinner any day of the week. I love it for that reason and also because of the affectionate nickname for spatchcocked birds in South Africa, chicken flatties! Since I only cook for two, a smaller, young chicken makes more sense for us, but the recipe can easily be doubled by using two young chickens if you're feeding a crowd—just bump up the broiling time accordingly.

1 (2½- to 3-pound) chicken

Kosher salt and freshly ground black pepper

4 tablespoons unsalted butter, softened

4 large garlic cloves, minced

1 tablespoon chopped fresh parsley

1 tablespoon chopped fresh chives

1 teaspoon chopped fresh thyme leaves

1 teaspoon ground coriander

1 small lemon, zested and cut into wedges for serving

1   To spatchcock the chicken, place it on a cutting board, skin side down. Starting at the thigh end, cut along each side of the backbone with sharp kitchen shears. Remove the backbone and reserve it for making stock. Flip the chicken over, and firmly press down on the breastbone with your hands to flatten it.

2   Transfer the chicken to a rimmed sheet pan. Season both sides with salt (I use 1 teaspoon per pound of chicken) and pepper and let sit, loosely covered, for 30 minutes to 1 hour at room temperature.

3   Preheat the oven to broil with a rack 8 to 10 inches from the broiler.

4   In a medium bowl, stir together the butter, garlic, parsley, chives, thyme, coriander, and lemon zest until well combined.

5   Pat the chicken dry with paper towels. Starting at the bottom, work your way up to gently separate the skin from the chicken breast. Rub 2 tablespoons of the herb butter under the skin. (Don't worry if you can't get it all the way down, just pat the skin back in place and move the butter around from the outside.)

6   Rub the remaining butter evenly all over the front and back of the chicken and broil, skin side down, until golden brown, 15 to 20 minutes. Flip the chicken and baste the skin with the melted butter and drippings. Continue to broil, basting the chicken occasionally, until an instant-read thermometer inserted into the thickest part of the breast reaches 165°F, 15 to 20 minutes more. Transfer the chicken to a serving platter and spoon over the juices in the sheet pan. Let rest for 5 minutes before carving, then serve with the lemon wedges.

Pesto Chicken with Options

Serves 4   Thighs are the best part of a chicken, and I prepare them a million different ways, changing it up based on what's in season. However, the method is always the same: season the chicken generously, let the seasoning penetrate the meat, and finally, sear the thighs before roasting in the oven for the crispiest skin. This highly adaptable dish is one of my very favorite ways to prepare them, served over pasta or polenta. Switch up the add-ons as you shift through the seasons, using the guide at the end of the recipe as inspiration.

4 bone-in skin-on chicken thighs
(about 2 pounds; see Notes)

1½ teaspoons kosher salt

4 garlic cloves, minced

½ cup dry white wine, such as Sauvignon Blanc

½ cup Chicken Stock (page 259) or low-sodium chicken broth

¼ cup basil pesto or sun-dried tomato pesto

Spring, Summer, Fall, or Winter vegetables
(options follow)

4 ounces sheep's milk feta cheese (see Notes),
broken into chunks

Chopped fresh herbs (any combination
of chives, parsley, thyme, basil and oregano leaves
for spring and summer; sage leaves and rosemary needles
for fall and winter), for garnish

¼ teaspoon red pepper flakes (optional)

1   Pat the chicken very dry using paper towels, then season on both sides with the salt. Let sit, covered, for 30 to 45 minutes at room temperature or up to overnight in the refrigerator for best results. If refrigerating, remove the chicken 1 hour before cooking.

2   Preheat the oven to 375°F with a rack in the center position.

3   In a large ovenproof skillet, place the chicken skin side down, and set over medium heat. (Starting the chicken in a cold pan renders the fat better, resulting in a crispier skin.) Cook, undisturbed, until the fat is rendered and the chicken skin is golden brown and crisp when tapped with a fork, 3 to 4 minutes. Flip and cook the other side until golden brown, another 3 to 4 minutes.

4   Transfer the chicken to a plate, and pour off all but 2 tablespoons of the rendered fat, then return the skillet to medium heat. Add the garlic and cook, stirring often, until fragrant, about 30 seconds. Add the wine and cook, stirring occasionally, until the liquid is reduced by half, about 2 minutes. Pour in the stock and stir in the pesto, then return the chicken to the skillet, skin side up. Arrange your vegetables of choice and the feta evenly around the thighs.

5   Transfer the skillet to the oven, and roast until the thickest part of the thigh close to the bone reaches 165°F on an instant-read thermometer, about 30 minutes.

6   Garnish with the fresh herbs, sprinkle with the red pepper flakes, if using, and serve.

Notes

To swap out the thighs for boneless skinless chicken breasts, skip the searing and roast directly with the vegetables in the skillet until the chicken reaches 165°F on an instant-read thermometer, 15 to 20 minutes depending on the thickness.

The feta can be replaced with heaped tablespoons of ricotta after the chicken comes out of the oven.

SPRING

1 (12-ounce) jar marinated artichoke hearts, drained

1 small bunch radish, topped and quartered

SUMMER

1 small bunch broccolini, tough ends trimmed

1 cup cherry tomatoes

FALL

2 cups Brussels sprouts, halved

1 small delicata squash, halved lengthwise, seeded, and cut into ½-inch-thick slices

WINTER

10 ounces cubed butternut squash

1 small red onion, cut into ½-inch wedges

Grilled Peanut Chicken Noodle Bowls

Serves 4   You'd most likely associate peanut sauce with Southeast Asian cuisine, with one of the most popular variations being Indonesian satay sauce. Here, I combine creamy peanut butter with my Everyday Gochujang Sauce (page 259) for a Korean-inspired twist on satay sauce that I use both to season the chicken and as a dressing for the noodles and crunchy vegetables in this speedy recipe. Though I'm not usually too big on boneless skinless chicken breasts, halving them into cutlets shortens the cooking time significantly and keeps them juicy. If you're pressed for time, there's no shame in serving up shredded rotisserie chicken breast tossed in 2 tablespoons of the sauce instead of cooking from scratch or using preshredded carrots to avoid any peeling or grating. Those matchstick carrots are more visually striking anyways!

¼ cup Everyday Gochujang Sauce (page 259)

¼ cup creamy peanut butter

2 tablespoons water, plus more if needed

4 ounces soba noodles

1 tablespoon avocado oil

2 (8-ounce) boneless skinless chicken breasts, each halved horizontally into cutlets

¾ teaspoon kosher salt

½ teaspoon freshly ground black pepper

½ large romaine lettuce head, cored and chopped (2 cups)

2 Persian cucumbers, halved lengthwise and sliced into half-moons

1 medium carrot, peeled and shredded (about ½ cup)

16 Peppadew peppers, halved (about 1 cup)

4 green onions, thinly sliced (about ½ cup)

½ cup loosely packed chopped fresh cilantro leaves

½ cup chopped roasted salted peanuts

Lime wedges, for serving (optional)

1   In a small bowl, combine the gochujang sauce, peanut butter, and water, and stir until smooth. Add more water to thin the sauce out to your desired consistency, if needed.

2   Bring a medium saucepan of water to a boil. Add the soba noodles and cook according to the package instructions. Drain and rinse under cold running water until completely cool, then transfer to a large bowl.

3   Meanwhile, in a large grill pan or skillet, heat the avocado oil over medium-high heat. Season the chicken with the salt and pepper and toss with 1 tablespoon of the peanut sauce. Transfer the chicken to the grill pan and cook until grill marks appear on the bottom, about 2½ minutes. Flip the chicken and cook until cooked through, about 2 minutes more. Transfer to a cutting board and let rest for 5 minutes, then chop into bite-size pieces.

4   Divide the noodles, lettuce, cucumbers, carrot, Peppadews, green onions, cilantro, peanuts, and chicken among bowls. Drizzle each bowl with a few tablespoons of the remaining peanut sauce, and serve with the lime wedges, if desired.

Garlic Peri-Peri Roast Chicken

Serves 4   I had my first whole roasted chicken after I left South Africa. Most times, the birds that my mother cooked were purchased already portioned because it was cheaper, and when we did happen to secure a whole chicken, she cut it up before cooking anyway, out of habit. I envied the American families on television shows like *The Wonder Years* and *Friends*, who proudly displayed their whole roasted chickens or turkeys during special dinners. I wanted to be the designated carver who'd slice into the breast with precision as people around the table oohed and aahed. It all seemed so festive and elegant!

In South Africa, chicken cooked with peri-peri sauce (also known as *piri-piri* or *pili-pili* sauce) is as much of a staple as barbecue is here in the American South. Peri-peri chicken is usually spatchcocked before marinating and cooked over a wood fire outside for an extra smoky flavor. While you could roast the chicken whole outdoors, you'd have to pay close attention to prevent the sauce from charring from the flare-ups. This easy oven-roasted method is a more hands-off approach that I keep in my back pocket for last-minute gatherings here in the States. The chicken is cooked and served whole for carving at the table, just like the showstoppers that intrigued my younger self.

1 whole chicken (3 to 4 pounds)

Kosher salt

Freshly ground black pepper

1 cup Garlic Peri-Peri Sauce (page 262), divided

1 lemon, cut into wedges

Fresh oregano, thyme, or rosemary sprigs, for garnish (optional)

1   Pat the chicken very dry with paper towels. Generously season the chicken inside and out all over with salt and pepper (I use 1 tablespoon salt and 1 teaspoon pepper). Put the chicken into a large zip-top plastic bag, and pour in ½ cup of the garlic peri-peri sauce. Massage the sauce all over the chicken, then squeeze as much air out of the bag as possible and seal. Refrigerate on a large plate for at least 3 hours, up to overnight. Remove from the refrigerator 45 minutes before cooking.

2   Preheat the oven to 425°F with a rack in the center position. Line a rimmed sheet pan with parchment paper.

3   Remove the chicken from the marinade, letting any excess drip off, and place it breast side up on the prepared sheet pan. Discard remaining marinade from bag. Roast until the thickest part of the thigh registers 165°F on an instant-read thermometer, 45 minutes to 1 hour (about 15 minutes per pound). Tent the chicken with foil if it gets too dark. Brush the chicken all over with the remaining ½ cup garlic peri-peri sauce.

4   Transfer the chicken to a platter. Serve with the lemon wedges and herb sprigs, if desired.

Chicken with Saucy Rosemary Beans

Serves 4   The first meal that my mother allowed me to cook for the family unsupervised was lemon pepper chicken. I seasoned the chicken portions thoroughly, placed them on a sheet pan, and then proceeded to cook them for one whole hour at the absolute incorrect oven temperature. The chicken was pale, rock-solid, and barely edible. Not wanting to waste, we plated it up and giggled at the table while trying to cut into the driest chicken known to man. Experience is the best teacher. This tried-and-true technique of searing chicken on the stovetop before roasting in the oven produces crispy, golden skin and juicy meat every time. The beans are cooked in the rendered schmaltz along with the Cajun holy trinity of onion, bell pepper, and celery for even more flavor. It's a cheap, healthy, no-fail dinner that even a less-experienced cook could prepare with ease.

LEMONY CHICKEN THIGHS

1 tablespoon extra-virgin olive oil

4 bone-in skin-on chicken thighs (1 to 1¼ pounds total)

1½ teaspoons Greek seasoning (I like Cavender's), or your favorite lemon pepper seasoning

½ teaspoon kosher salt

SAUCY ROSEMARY BEANS

1 cup finely diced yellow onion

½ cup finely diced celery

½ cup finely diced red bell pepper

1 tablespoon minced garlic

1 teaspoon minced fresh rosemary

¾ teaspoon kosher salt

½ teaspoon freshly ground black pepper

2 (15.5-ounce) cans cannellini or other white beans, drained and rinsed

2 cups Chicken Stock (page 259) or low-sodium chicken broth

1 fresh bay leaf

4 cups fresh baby spinach

FOR SERVING

1 small lemon, quartered

1   TO COOK THE CHICKEN, rub the olive oil over the chicken thighs and sprinkle them all over with the Greek seasoning. Cover and let the chicken sit at room temperature for 30 minutes.

2   Preheat the oven to 375°F with a rack in the center position.

3   In a large saucepan over medium-high heat, place the chicken, skin side down, and cook, flipping halfway through, until the skin is light golden and crisp when tapped with a fork, 3 to 5 minutes per side. Transfer the chicken to a rimmed sheet pan and roast in the oven for about 20 minutes, until a digital thermometer inserted into the thickest part reads 165°F. Reserve the saucepan with the chicken juices.

4   TO MAKE THE SAUCY BEANS, heat the juices in the saucepan over medium heat. Add the onion, celery, red bell pepper, garlic, rosemary, salt, and black pepper, and cook, stirring, until the onion is soft and light golden brown, 5 to 8 minutes. Add the beans, chicken stock, and bay leaf, and cook, covered, stirring occasionally, until the flavors have melded, about 15 minutes. Reduce the heat to low, and use a fork to mash some of the beans on the side of the saucepan for a creamier consistency, if desired. Stir in the spinach and cover until wilted, about 2 minutes. Discard the bay leaf.

5   FOR SERVING, divide the beans among four shallow bowls. Top each with a roasted chicken thigh and place the lemon wedges on the table for everyone to squeeze over their bowls.

Creamy Chicken Livers on Toast

Serves 4   Without a doubt, this is on my list of top five things to eat! You can find peri-peri-spiced chicken livers as an appetizer on 90 percent of menus in South Africa, with Portuguese bread rolls (*papo secos*) and real butter on the side. Stateside, I enjoy it for breakfast or dinner, but I'm very particular about the way I eat it: Hot chicken livers with sauce spooned over toasted bread spread with a thick slab of cold grass-fed butter. The savory sauce melts into the butter, letting the flavors meld, and it's a mouthful gone to heaven. I garnish the toasts with an easy pickled carrot salad similar to what you'd find in Vietnamese banh mi. It adds a welcome freshness and acidity to the rich chicken livers. If you were on the fence before, try them this way and you might just change your mind.

PICKLED CARROTS

2 medium carrots, peeled and julienned (I like colorful heirloom varieties)

2 tablespoons rice wine vinegar

1 tablespoon sugar

CHICKEN LIVERS

1 tablespoon salted grass-fed butter

1 tablespoon extra-virgin olive oil

1 small yellow onion, finely chopped

4 garlic cloves, minced

1 pound fresh chicken livers, trimmed of excess fat

¼ cup fresh lemon juice

2 tablespoons tomato paste

½ tablespoon Worcestershire sauce

1½ teaspoons ground cumin

1½ teaspoons smoked paprika

1 teaspoon peri-peri chili powder or ½ teaspoon minced fresh red chili

1 teaspoon kosher salt

2 fresh bay leaves

½ cup heavy cream

1 tablespoon brandy (optional)

FOR SERVING

4 thick slices crusty bread

4 tablespoons salted grass-fed butter

¼ cup loosely packed fresh cilantro leaves

1   TO MAKE THE PICKLED CARROTS, in a medium bowl, toss together the carrots, vinegar, and sugar until well coated. Refrigerate until ready to serve.

2   TO COOK THE CHICKEN LIVERS, in a large skillet, heat the butter and oil over medium heat. Add the onion and garlic, and cook, stirring, until the onion is light golden brown and the garlic is fragrant, 3 to 5 minutes. Add the chicken livers, lemon juice, tomato paste, Worcestershire sauce, cumin, paprika, peri-peri chili powder, salt, and bay leaves. Cook, stirring occasionally, until the chicken livers are evenly coated and browned, 2 to 3 minutes. Reduce the heat to medium-low, then pour in the heavy cream and stir until the chicken livers are just cooked through but still slightly pink in the middle, 3 to 4 minutes. (I usually test one by cutting it open in the skillet.) Stir in the brandy, if using, and remove the skillet from the heat. Discard the bay leaves.

3   TO SERVE, toast the bread, and spread each slice with 1 tablespoon of the butter. Spoon a generous amount of the chicken livers on top, adding enough sauce to soak into the bread, then finish the toasts with the pickled carrots and cilantro leaves.

Mom's Red Beans with Smoked Turkey

Serves 8   The first home-cooked Southern meal that I ate in America was red beans and rice. My mother-in-love, Iscinova, took me under her wing and taught me how to prepare their treasured family recipe the moment that I walked through her front door. It felt lovely to know that I could fall right in and help around the house, and I appreciated her matter-of-fact sensibility. "We only use Camellia red beans in this house," she said, as she opened the package and poured it into the pot of soft-cooked holy trinity of onions, bell pepper, and celery. "We don't eat pork so I use smoked turkey sausage and smoked turkey. You won't even miss any andouille," she said. She was right! It's one of our favorite meals to make when we want a taste of Mom's home cooking. My only change is a dash of fresh lemon juice at the end, and die-hard red beans and rice experts may take issue with this addition, but trust me! It gives the hearty beans and smoked meats just enough freshness and zing.

4 tablespoons unsalted butter

2 cups chopped yellow onion

1 cup chopped green bell pepper

1 cup chopped celery ("with leaves, for flavor!" Mom says)

2 tablespoons minced garlic

1 pound smoked turkey sausage, cut into
¼-inch-thick slices, divided

1½ to 2 pounds smoked turkey wing pieces

1 pound dried red kidney beans, soaked overnight in water, drained

2 fresh bay leaves

12 cups Chicken Stock (page 259), low-sodium chicken broth, or water, divided

¼ cup chopped fresh parsley

2 tablespoons fresh lemon juice

1½ tablespoons Creole Seasoning (page 256) or store-bought Cajun blend

1 tablespoon freshly ground black pepper

FOR SERVING

1 tablespoon extra-virgin olive oil

8 cups cooked long-grain rice

Celery leaves, for garnish

Hot sauce (optional)

1   In a large Dutch oven over medium-high heat, melt the butter. Add the onion, bell pepper, celery, and garlic, and cook, stirring occasionally, until the vegetables just start to soften and the garlic is fragrant, 3 to 5 minutes. Add half the sausage and cook, stirring occasionally, until the sausage is evenly browned, 2 to 3 minutes. Add the turkey, beans, bay leaves, and 10 cups of the stock, pushing the turkey down if necessary to submerge it in the liquid. Bring to a rolling boil, then reduce the heat to medium and cook, covered, stirring occasionally and skimming the foam from the surface as needed, until the beans are tender and the turkey is falling off the bone, 1½ to 2 hours. If the beans look too dry before they are tender, stir in 1 to 2 more cups of the remaining stock and continue to cook.

2   Reduce the heat to low, then shred the turkey wings, discarding the bones and any large pieces of skin. Discard the bay leaves. Use a potato masher or fork to mash half of the beans, and stir in the parsley, lemon juice, Creole seasoning, and black pepper.

3   TO SERVE, in a medium skillet, heat the olive oil over medium-high heat. Add the remaining sausage and cook, stirring often, until golden brown and crisp, about 1 minute.

4   Spoon some of the red beans into bowls with the rice and top with the crisped sausage. Garnish with the celery leaves and offer some hot sauce on the side, if using.

Fridge Raid Grilled Chicken Board

Serves 4 You might know the feeling: Evening is approaching and though you've thought about what to eat all day, nothing seems to come together. Suddenly someone asks, "What's for dinner?" and now it's a race to figure something out before anyone gets too hangry. High stress! Just me?

It's easy to give up and order dinner in an age when takeout is just a swipe away. Sometimes (most times, twice a week) these spiced and grilled chicken thighs are the final frontier before I resort to the delivery apps. Real talk. The chicken is coated with a few basic spices with zero time marinating because sometimes even ten minutes is too long. What sets them apart is a quick toss in lemon juice and maple syrup right after they come out of the air fryer, grill pan, or skillet. The chicken is a perfect topper for almost anything, from crispy fries, salads, and ramen to grain or rice bowls. In the spirit of not wasting what can be salvaged, I raid the refrigerator for suitable accompaniments. That might be some leftover dips, a few pickly things, and vegetable stragglers hanging out in the crisper. Alone in the refrigerator, these ingredients might not look like much, but when composed on a big board with the chicken, they complete a perfect dinner puzzle in no time at all. Look at the masterpiece you just created, the waste you just reduced, and the money you just saved by avoiding takeout.

CHICKEN

2 tablespoons extra-virgin olive oil

1½ teaspoons paprika

1½ teaspoons kosher salt

1 teaspoon freshly ground black pepper, plus more for serving (optional)

1 teaspoon garlic powder

1 teaspoon chipotle chili powder

1 teaspoon ground cumin

1 teaspoon dried thyme

2 pounds boneless skinless chicken thighs, trimmed

Grated zest and juice of 1 lemon

1 tablespoon pure maple syrup or honey

FOR SERVING (OPTIONAL)

½ cup your favorite hummus

½ cup Yogurt Feta Sauce (page 263)

Pita wedges

Sliced cucumbers

Cherry tomatoes

Quartered radishes

Small lettuce leaves

Sliced red onion

Olives

Pickled peppers

Lemon wedges

Fresh mint sprigs, for garnish

1 COOK THE CHICKEN: In a large bowl, whisk together the olive oil, paprika, salt, pepper, garlic powder, chili powder, cumin, and thyme until well combined. Add the chicken and toss until well coated on both sides. I massage everything by hand, for good measure.

2 STOVETOP METHOD: Heat a large grill pan or cast-iron skillet over medium heat. Add the chicken thighs and cook, flipping once, until grill marks appear or the chicken is deep golden brown and cooked through, 4 to 5 minutes per side.

3 AIR FRYER METHOD: Preheat the air fryer to 375°F. Working in batches if necessary, add the chicken in a single layer and cook, undisturbed, until golden brown on both sides and cooked through, about 8 minutes per batch.

4 In a large bowl, stir together the lemon zest, lemon juice, and maple syrup until well combined. Slice the chicken, add it to the bowl, and gently toss to coat. Transfer to a serving board and sprinkle with pepper, if desired.

5 FOR SERVING: Arrange any of the accompaniments around the chicken and garnish with mint sprigs.

Oven-Roasted "Barbecue" Chicken with a Greek(ish) Wedge

Serves 4   When I think of barbecue chicken, the fire-grilled marinated chicken that my parents cooked and sold to raise money for charity comes to mind. We called it barbecue or braai chicken solely because of the cooking method, and not because barbecue sauce was involved. On fundraising weekends, Dad would marinate up to two hundred chicken legs at a time with his special blend of vinegar and spices, then grill it outside with my uncles, while getting tipsy off brandy and Coca-Cola. Once the chicken was perfectly cooked, the women formed an assembly line to plate each piece in a Styrofoam container with a dinner roll, Mom's curried noodle salad, and a Greek salad assembled right on the spot. Neighbors, friends, and family alike were huge fans of these barbecued chicken plates and spread word of the good eats like wildfire until we sold out completely. One year, in 2000, the chicken plates even helped me raise enough money to be second runner-up in the church debutante pageant, so it must've been good! While my slow-roasted oven version here isn't an exact replica of Dad's secret recipe (he never measured), the piquant flavor that my marinade gives the chicken hits really close to home. I serve it with a pared-down Greek salad, assembled right on the plate, before digging in.

CHICKEN

⅓ cup extra-virgin olive oil

⅓ cup red wine vinegar

½ small yellow onion, grated (about 2 tablespoons)

4 garlic cloves, minced

1 tablespoon Worcestershire sauce

1 tablespoon ketchup

2 teaspoons kosher salt

1 teaspoon smoked paprika

1 teaspoon dry mustard powder

1 teaspoon finely ground black pepper

1 teaspoon ground cumin

4 chicken leg quarters (3 to 3½ pounds)

GREEK(ISH) WEDGE

1 small iceberg lettuce head, cut into 1-inch-thick slabs

1 cup whole-milk Greek yogurt

1 cup cherry tomatoes, halved

2 Persian cucumbers, thinly sliced

¼ red onion, halved and thinly sliced

⅓ cup pitted olives, halved lengthwise

Fresh basil or other soft herbs, such as dill fronds or oregano leaves, for garnish

Flaky salt and freshly ground black pepper

1   TO ROAST THE CHICKEN, in a large resealable bowl, combine the olive oil, vinegar, onion, garlic, Worcestershire sauce, ketchup, salt, smoked paprika, mustard powder, pepper, and cumin; whisk together until the marinade is emulsified. Pour off ¼ cup of the marinade and set aside for basting. Add the chicken to the remaining marinade and toss until fully coated. Cover and refrigerate for at least 1 hour, up to overnight. Remove the chicken 1 hour before cooking.

2   Preheat the oven to 325°F with a rack in the center position.

3   Transfer the chicken, skin side up, to a large, rimmed sheet pan, letting any excess marinade drip back into the bowl; discard this marinade. Roast, flipping and basting with the reserved marinade and pan juices halfway through, until the thickest part of the chicken reaches 165°F on an instant-read thermometer, about 50 minutes to 1 hour, depending on the size (see Note). Transfer the chicken to plates.

4   TO ASSEMBLE A WEDGE SALAD WITH EACH CHICKEN LEG, start with a slab of lettuce, then dollop a few tablespoons of the yogurt on top, and finish with the tomatoes, cucumbers, red onion, and olives, dividing evenly. Garnish with basil, sprinkle with flaky salt and pepper, and serve any extra yogurt on the side.

Note

Test the chicken for doneness by inserting an instant-read thermometer sideways into the thickest part between the leg and thigh, making sure to not touch the bone. The chicken is cooked when the temperature reaches 165°F, but I like to take it even further to 185°F for fall-off-the-bone tender chicken.

four

BEEF

Grilled Short Ribs with Pickled Radish (Galbi)

Serves 4 So much Korean food is comfort food to me, especially sweet and savory, grilled meaty dishes with an array of vegetable side dishes (*banchan*) served alongside. Once upon a time, I knew nothing about South Korea, its location on a world map, or what I would face if I moved there, but I took a chance and fell deeply in love with the cuisine and culture. Now, I take every opportunity to cook and eat Korean-inspired meals with my family.

The word *galbi* translates to English as "ribs," and flanken-style ribs have become synonymous with Korean barbecue. Cut crosswise through the rib bones, the thin strips of meat are longer, thinner, and perfect for marinating and grilling. The meat soaks up the flavor of a sweet, soy-based marinade before sizzling over hot charcoal grills inlaid into tables at Korean barbecue restaurants. DJ and I have traveled to different states just for a taste, but this simplified at-home version is always on our dinner rotation.

When it comes to side dishes, we love a variety of colors and textures on the table. I serve my short ribs with quick pickled radish, perilla leaves (sometimes sold as "sesame leaves" in Korean grocery stores), green chili, kimchi, ssamjang, and sesame oil with toasted sesame seeds for dipping. The short ribs are also delicious with a bowl of steamed rice.

SHORT RIBS

¼ cup soy sauce

¼ cup sesame oil

2 tablespoons brown sugar

2 tablespoons minced garlic

1 tablespoon finely grated, peeled fresh ginger

2 teaspoons freshly ground black pepper

3 pounds flanken-style short ribs (see Notes)

PICKLED RADISH (SEE NOTES)

1 bunch radishes, tops removed and quartered

1 tablespoon rice wine vinegar

2 teaspoons granulated sugar

½ teaspoon kosher salt

FOR SERVING (OPTIONAL)

24 perilla leaves (see Notes)

½ cup sliced jalapeño or serrano chile

½ cup store-bought kimchi or Easy Mak Kimchi (page 260)

½ cup ssamjang or Miso Tahini Sauce (page 262)

2 tablespoons sesame oil

1 teaspoon roasted sesame seeds

1   To marinate the short ribs, in a large zip-top plastic bag, combine the soy sauce, sesame oil, brown sugar, garlic, ginger, and pepper. Add the short ribs, seal the bag, and turn to coat. Marinate for 1 hour at room temperature or refrigerate up to overnight and remove from the fridge 1 hour before cooking.

2   Meanwhile, to make the pickled radish, in a small bowl, combine the radishes, vinegar, sugar, and salt. Stir and refrigerate until ready to serve.

3   Heat a grill or griddle to medium-high heat.

4   Remove the short ribs from the marinade, letting any excess marinade drip off. Grill in a single layer, undisturbed, until the fat is rendered and the meat is slightly charred around the edges, about 2 minutes per side. Transfer the short ribs to a platter and serve with the pickled radish, perilla leaves, chile, kimchi, ssamjang or miso tahini sauce, sesame oil, and sesame seeds, if desired.

Notes

Since flanken-style short ribs are cut through the bone it's not unusual to see small bone fragments on them. To remove them, rinse the short ribs under cold, running water and pat them very dry before marinating.

If you prefer, packages of ready-to-serve pickled daikon radish wraps can be purchased from the refrigerated section at most Asian grocery stores.

Perilla leaves can be hard to track down depending on the time of year. Sturdy green leaf lettuce leaves won't tear easily when wrapping and make a great substitute.

Mom's Meatballs in Tomato Gravy (Tamatie Frikkadel)

Serves 4   This recipe, adapted by the Cape Malay people in South Africa, was originally brought to the Cape via Dutch settlers. It's as old as time and has been passed down from my grandmother to my mother, and now to me. I treasure it and consider it to be the ultimate *huiskos* (the Afrikaans word for "weeknight meal") because it uses ingredients that I always have on hand. The fresh ginger and ground cloves give the meatballs and gravy a subtle warmth that tastes like home to me (most tomato-based dishes I grew up with are redolent with these aromatics). Think of the recipe as a South African version of Italian meatballs in gravy! You might be tempted to use bread crumbs instead of the milk-soaked bread here, but it's essential for incredibly tender, light, and tasty meatballs, so just know that they might turn out denser if you choose another route. Pair them with steamed rice, pasta, mashed potatoes, or polenta.

2 slices white or brown sandwich bread, roughly torn

¼ cup whole milk

2 large yellow onions, quartered

1 large green bell pepper, stem and seeds removed

8 large garlic cloves, minced

1 pound lean ground beef

1 large egg

¼ cup finely chopped fresh parsley

1 tablespoon grated peeled fresh ginger

1½ teaspoons kosher salt

1 teaspoon freshly ground black pepper

¼ teaspoon ground cloves

1 tablespoon extra-virgin olive oil

1½ cups Chicken Stock (page 259) or low-sodium chicken broth, or water

¼ cup tomato paste

1½ tablespoons sugar

1   Place the bread in a shallow bowl, and cover with the milk. Let the milk soak in, then use a fork to mash the bread into a very fine pulp. Soaking the bread in the milk is an important step to ensure juicy meatballs.

2   In a food processor, combine the onions, bell pepper, and garlic. Process until finely chopped. Reserve half for the tomato gravy; transfer the rest to a large bowl and add the beef, egg, parsley, ginger, salt, pepper, and ground cloves. Add the mashed bread and mix by hand until well blended. Cover and refrigerate.

3   Meanwhile, in a large saucepan or skillet heat the olive oil over medium heat. Add the reserved onion mixture and cook, stirring occasionally, until the onions are light golden brown and soft, 5 to 6 minutes. Stir in the chicken stock, tomato paste, and sugar. Reduce the heat to medium-low, and simmer, stirring occasionally, while you form the meatballs.

4   Form the meatball mixture into eight meatballs, carefully adding each one to the sauce as you go. Cover and cook, carefully flipping once halfway through, until the meatballs are fully cooked, and the sauce is slightly reduced, 10 to 12 minutes (see Note).

Note

Be gentle when flipping the meatballs in the saucepan because they are delicate. I use a fork and soup spoon to make this task easier.

Birthday Beef Cheeks
with Preserved Lemon Gremolata

Serves 4   If you walk down Royal Street in New Orleans, you'll most likely pass by Sylvain, a quaint restaurant down a narrow alley with a dark interior and intimate courtyard. I've celebrated my birthday there every year since first tasting the braised beef cheeks with potato puree. It's an unforgettable plate made with an underrated cut of meat often labeled as organ meat by retailers due to more sinew or silverskin than premium cuts. However, with a little time in the oven, this seemingly lowbrow working muscle transforms into a beautifully tender braise fit for royalty. In this re-creation of that cherished birthday meal, I lean on ingredients like nutmeg, allspice, horseradish, and preserved lemons to highlight the beef cheek. It's a celebration with every forkful!

BEEF CHEEKS
2 pounds beef cheeks, trimmed of silverskin and patted dry (see Note)

1 tablespoon Dijon mustard

2 tablespoons cornstarch

1 tablespoon finely chopped fresh rosemary needles

1½ teaspoons kosher salt

1 teaspoon freshly ground black pepper

½ teaspoon ground coriander

¼ teaspoon ground nutmeg

¼ teaspoon ground allspice

2 tablespoons extra-virgin olive oil

1 large yellow onion, diced

8 ounces cremini mushrooms, trimmed of tough ends and sliced

1 cup diced celery

½ cup diced red bell pepper

8 large garlic cloves, minced

⅓ cup brandy or whiskey

3 cups Chicken Stock (page 259) or low-sodium chicken broth

PRESERVED LEMON GREMOLATA
½ cup finely chopped fresh parsley

2 tablespoons finely chopped rind from preserved lemons, homemade (page 258) or store-bought

1 garlic clove, minced

HERBY HORSERADISH MASHED POTATOES
2 pounds russet potatoes, peeled and cut into 1-inch cubes

1 tablespoon kosher salt

1 cup heavy cream, half-and-half, buttermilk, or milk

1 tablespoon prepared horseradish or 1½ teaspoons horseradish powder

8 tablespoons (1 stick) unsalted butter, divided

1 tablespoon chopped fresh chives

1 tablespoon chopped fresh parsley

1   Preheat the oven to 325°F with a rack in the center position.

2   TO PREPARE THE BEEF CHEEKS, in a large bowl, combine the beef with the mustard until evenly coated. Sprinkle with the cornstarch, rosemary, salt, pepper, coriander, nutmeg, and allspice, tossing to coat.

3   In a large Dutch oven or braiser, heat the oil over medium-high heat. When the oil shimmers, working in batches, add the beef cheeks in a single layer with enough space between them to brown evenly and cook until deep golden brown, about 3 minutes per side. Transfer to a plate.

4   To the same skillet, add the onion, mushrooms, celery, bell pepper, and garlic, and cook over medium heat, stirring occasionally, until the onion is translucent and the mushrooms have decreased in volume, 5 to 8 minutes (if the mixture becomes too dry, add up to ¼ cup water to prevent sticking). Add the brandy and stir, scraping any browned bits off the bottom of the pot with a wooden spoon, until almost all the liquid evaporates, about 1 minute. Return the beef to the pot, pour in the chicken stock, and cover. Cook in the oven until the beef is very tender, 3 to 3½ hours.

continues on page 141

5   TO MAKE THE GREMOLATA, in a small bowl, stir together the parsley, preserved lemon rind, and garlic. Set aside or refrigerate until ready to serve.

6   TO MAKE THE MASHED POTATOES, in a large pot, combine the potatoes and salt with enough water to cover the potatoes by 1 inch. Bring to a boil over medium-high heat and cook, partially covered, until fork-tender, 15 to 20 minutes.

7   Drain the potatoes, then return them to the empty pot over low heat. Add the heavy cream, horseradish, and 6 tablespoons of the butter. Using a potato masher, mash the potatoes until completely smooth, 1 to 2 minutes. Stir in the chives and parsley, and transfer to a serving bowl. Press the remaining 2 tablespoons butter into the middle of the warm potatoes and serve hot.

8   Ladle the beef cheeks and gravy over the mashed potatoes, and top with the gremolata.

Note

These days it's commonplace for butchers to trim meat according to a recipe's specifications, so don't be afraid to ask and get a head start on prep! If you're unable to find beef cheeks, then beef chuck, short ribs, or well-marbled stewing beef are all great alternatives.

Not an Italian Grandma's Cheesy Lasagna

Serves 6   The meat sauce in this recipe isn't complicated and doesn't pretend to be something else. It has always been there in times when my grandmother knew she had to feed my cousins and me something that we would actually eat after school. She used what she had in her pantry to create it, but her hand was heavy and she often over-seasoned with pepper. Despite that, her peppery sauce is what my cousins and I came to love and crave, even though we are now spread out around the world, more than twenty years later. Grandma used whole cloves, and they aren't really optional because it's what adds that signature South African flavor to savory meat dishes—just be sure to scoop them out when the sauce is done. I can't tell you how many times she forgot and had one of us very shocked after biting into one.

While grandma served her sauce with spaghetti, I love it in this easy, cheesy, baked lasagna.

Olive oil spray, for greasing

1 tablespoon extra-virgin olive oil

1 medium yellow onion, finely chopped

1 pound extra-lean ground beef

4 large garlic cloves, minced

1 (28-ounce) can crushed tomatoes

1 cup water

1½ tablespoons sugar

1 tablespoon tomato paste

1 tablespoon Worcestershire sauce

1 tablespoon Italian seasoning

2 teaspoons freshly ground black pepper, plus more for serving (optional)

1 teaspoon kosher salt

4 whole cloves

1 fresh bay leaf

¼ cup finely chopped fresh parsley, plus 1 tablespoon for serving

1 (15-ounce) container whole-milk ricotta

1 pound whole-milk mozzarella cheese, shredded

1 large egg, beaten

1 (9-ounce) package oven-ready lasagna noodles

¼ cup freshly grated aged Gouda or Parmesan cheese

1   Preheat the oven to 350°F with a rack in the center position. Lightly grease a 9 × 13-inch baking dish with olive oil spray.

2   In a large Dutch oven, heat the olive oil over medium heat. Add the onion and cook, stirring occasionally, until light golden and fragrant, 6 to 8 minutes. Add the ground beef and cook, breaking up any large pieces, until evenly browned, 4 to 5 minutes. Add the garlic, crushed tomatoes, water, sugar, tomato paste, Worcestershire sauce, Italian seasoning, pepper, salt, cloves, bay leaf, and ¼ cup parsley. Cook, covered, stirring occasionally, until the flavors meld and the sauce is thickened slightly, about 15 minutes. Remove and discard the cloves and the bay leaf.

3   While the sauce cooks, in a large bowl, stir together the ricotta, mozzarella, and egg until well combined.

4   In the prepared baking dish, layer the meat sauce, lasagna noodles, and ricotta mixture, dividing evenly, until you've used up all the ingredients, finishing with the layer of ricotta. Sprinkle the Gouda over the top. The layers don't need to be precise!

5   Bake until the lasagna is bubbling and golden brown in spots, 35 to 40 minutes. Sprinkle with the remaining 1 tablespoon parsley and extra black pepper, if desired.

Peppadew-Pimento Juicy Lucy Burgers

Serves 6   The "home" burgers of my youth were simple, made with preshaped patties purchased from the more upmarket grocery store, Woolworths, usually on Fridays toward the end of the month. The patties came in a pack of six, and we were a family of five, so there was usually one left that everyone wanted but nobody felt comfortable enough to ask for. We gave it to the dog to be fair because Biscuit really did deserve it.

You'll get six generously sized burgers out of this batch of my most requested "home" burgers, enough for a substantial meal, plus a few extra just in case. Instead of just making regular cheeseburgers, I like to stuff my burgers with cheese, inspired by the classic Juicy Lucy burger first invented in Minnesota. Initially, I made them with hoop cheese, an affordable mild variety similar to Cheddar available at any respectable Southern grocery store, then I started playing around with another Southern staple, pimento cheese, which made them next-level delicious. People undoubtedly request these when I ask, "What shall I cook?" and I'm very happy to oblige.

2 pounds ground beef chuck (80% lean/20% fat ratio)

1 tablespoon mild hot sauce

2 teaspoons kosher salt

2 teaspoons freshly ground black pepper

6 tablespoons Peppadew & Gouda Pimento Cheese (page 48) or your favorite store-bought pimento cheese

Avocado oil, for the grill or grill pan

FOR SERVING
6 brioche burger buns

Mayonnaise

Yellow or Dijon mustard

Ketchup

6 slices of your favorite cheese

1 head butter lettuce, leaves separated

1 large ripe beefsteak tomato, thinly sliced

½ red onion, thinly sliced into rings

Dill pickle slices

1   In a large bowl, combine the beef, hot sauce, salt, and pepper. Gently mix by hand, picking up the meat and sprinkling it back into the bowl. Avoid overworking or packing the meat down, which can result in tough burgers.

2   Divide the mixture into six meatballs, each weighing about 5½ ounces. Form the balls into patties, then make a well in the center of each one and add 1 tablespoon of the pimento cheese to each well. Pick each patty up, and carefully wrap the meat around the cheese to fully encase it, then flatten into a 1-inch-thick patty. Transfer the stuffed patties to a baking sheet, cover, and refrigerate for 30 minutes or up to overnight.

3   Grease a grill with avocado oil and heat to medium. Alternatively, in a grill pan, heat 1 tablespoon of avocado oil over medium heat. (I don't believe that grill marks are super important for things like burgers that will be sandwiched in a bun anyways. Low and slow is the way to go here, otherwise the meat will contract too quickly and force out the cheese.)

4   Cook the burgers, flipping once, until the cheese is melted and an instant-read thermometer inserted into each burger horizontally from the side reaches 145°F for medium doneness, 5 to 7 minutes per side. (Ensure the thermometer is inserted into the meat, not the cheese.)

5   Serve the burgers family-style with the buns, mayonnaise, mustard, ketchup, sliced cheese, lettuce, tomato, onion, and pickles.

SOUTH OF SOMEWHERE

PEPPADEW-PIMENTO JUICY LUCY BURGERS, 143

Grilled Bavette Steak
with Watermelon & Halloumi Salad

Serves 4 Don't get my husband, DJ, started talking about Tabasco. If you're not careful, he could go on and on about the hot sauce and his school field trips to the iconic factory on Avery Island, then soon you might find yourself searching for an escape. The love is so strong that he seems to be offended when Tabasco is not on offer at restaurants when we dine out. All jokes aside, I can totally understand his passion for the fiery sauce. It's become a staple in my kitchen, and particularly delicious in marinades like the one for this bavette steak, one of my all-time favorite cuts of beef. It's a very forgiving, flavorful cut with a relaxed texture that can handle robust seasonings, marinades, and slightly longer cooking times without drying out. While we grill just enough for the two of us, a whole bavette can weigh roughly three to four pounds, making it a great option if you're feeding a crowd—just increase the amount of marinade accordingly. Depending on your location, it's also known as flap steak, or fajita meat, but if you can't find it, don't fret, just use skirt or flank steak instead.

BAVETTE STEAK
¼ cup extra-virgin olive oil

2 tablespoons fresh lemon juice

1 tablespoon Tabasco sauce

1 large garlic clove, minced

1½ teaspoons ground coriander

1 teaspoon smoked paprika

Kosher salt and freshly ground black pepper

1 (1½-pound) bavette steak (about 1½ inches thick)

WATERMELON & HALLOUMI SALAD
8 ounces halloumi cheese, sliced ¼ inch thick

1 pound seedless watermelon, cut into ¼-inch pieces

¼ small red onion, thinly sliced

2 tablespoons fresh lemon juice

1 tablespoon honey (optional)

¼ cup roughly chopped fresh basil leaves

¼ cup loosely packed torn fresh mint leaves

1 TO MARINATE THE BAVETTE, in a large zip-top plastic bag, combine the olive oil, lemon juice, Tabasco, garlic, coriander, and paprika. Season with 1½ teaspoons salt and 1½ teaspoons pepper (1 teaspoon of each per pound of meat). Add the steak, seal the bag, and turn to coat. Marinate for 1 hour at room temperature or refrigerate up to overnight and remove from the refrigerator 1 to 2 hours before cooking.

2 Meanwhile, heat a grill to medium heat.

3 Remove the steak from the bag, letting excess marinade drip off. Grill, flipping occasionally, until the thickest part of the meat reaches 135°F on an instant-read thermometer for medium-rare, 6 to 7 minutes per side depending on the thickness of your steak. Transfer to a cutting board, tent loosely with foil, and let rest for 10 minutes.

4 MEANWHILE, TO MAKE THE SALAD, heat a medium, dry skillet over medium heat. Add the halloumi and cook, flipping halfway through, until golden brown and warmed through, about 1 minute per side.

5 Arrange the watermelon and onion on a large serving platter, then drizzle with the lemon juice. Top with the halloumi slices, then drizzle with the honey, if using, and sprinkle with the basil and mint.

6 Slice the steak against the grain (see Note on page 161), and serve with the salad.

Bobotie

Serves 6   Bobotie, an egg custard–topped spiced casserole, is one of the finest examples of Cape Malay cookery in South Africa, a true representation of the melting pot of cultures that inspired our cuisine. Though the transition seems to be mostly undocumented, the original can be traced back to the Javanese dish *bobotok*, which first made its way to Cape Town as far back as the seventeenth century when my ancestors were brought to South Africa as slaves. (For more about this history, see page 20.)

Cape Malay cooks gradually adapted the bobotok by adding fruit and vinegar to tame the heat for a more fragrant, mildly spiced version—making bobotie what it is today, a richly comforting dish that's savory, sweet, and spicy all at once. I like to make mine for guests who are curious enough to try something different and want to know more about the traditional foods I grew up eating.

1 teaspoon unsalted butter, for greasing

1¼ cups whole milk or coconut milk

2 slices white bread, roughly torn

1 tablespoon extra-virgin olive oil

1 large yellow onion, finely chopped

2 pounds extra-lean ground beef

6 large garlic cloves, minced

¼ cup golden raisins or grated fresh apple

¼ cup Mrs. H.S. Ball's Peach Chutney (available online), District Six Apricot Chutney (page 263), or any fruit chutney

1½ tablespoons mild curry powder (see Note)

1 tablespoon Worcestershire sauce

1 tablespoon fresh lemon juice

2 teaspoons ground turmeric

2 teaspoons kosher salt

1 teaspoon freshly cracked black pepper

⅛ teaspoon ground cloves

6 fresh lemon leaves or bay leaves

2 large eggs

Toasted slivered almonds, for serving (optional)

1   Preheat the oven to 350°F with a rack in the center position. Grease a 9-inch round, or 2½-quart, baking dish with the butter.

2   In a shallow bowl, pour the milk over the bread. Set aside and allow the milk to soak in.

3   In a large saucepan, heat the olive oil over medium heat. Add the onion and cook, stirring occasionally, until light golden brown, 4 to 5 minutes. Add the beef and garlic, and cook, stirring occasionally, until the meat is browned, 5 to 6 minutes. Pour off the excess fat.

4   Meanwhile, squeeze the excess milk out of the bread and add it to the skillet; reserve the milk. Add the raisins, chutney, curry powder, Worcestershire sauce, lemon juice, turmeric, salt, pepper, and cloves, and cook, stirring occasionally, and breaking up any lumps of beef or bread, until the flavors have melded and the sauce is thickened, about 5 minutes. Transfer to the prepared baking dish, then gently smooth the surface and arrange the lemon leaves in a pattern on top.

5   Beat the eggs into the reserved milk with a fork. Pour over the cooked beef, then bake until the custard is set and the edges of the bobotie just start to turn a light golden brown, about 30 minutes. Sprinkle with toasted slivered almonds, if desired. Your house should now be filled with the aroma that drifted through the narrow streets of my neighborhood every time someone decided to make this meal.

Note

Not all curry powders are created equal. Once you find a blend that you like, stash it in the freezer to keep it fresher for longer. I squirrel pounds of the good stuff away after trips to Cape Town, purchased from Atlas Trading in District Six, an established Cape Malay community on the slopes of Table Mountain. The bags keep for a year in my freezer, but I ran out during the pandemic when travel wasn't an option. In my search for something equivalent from a US purveyor, I found the Vadouvan curry powder from The Spice House to be the closest to the fruity, mild blends used in South Africa. Alternatively, check Amazon or the international aisle of bigger grocery stores for Rajah curry and pick up the yellow box.

Green Bean Stew (Groenboontjie Bredie)

Serves 4   I learned to cook this traditional South African stew by sitting at the kitchen counter, bright-eyed and bushy-tailed, carefully observing my mother and grandmother making it from start to finish. I like to think of it as the South African version of pot roast, a slightly old-fashioned yet comforting meal that makes everyone at the table so happy. The stew is typically made with lamb knuckles, but here in the US, my go-to is deeply flavorful cross-cut beef shin for the bone marrow, a key element that adds flavor to the gravy. It's a relatively inexpensive cut and becomes meltingly tender once fully cooked in the peppery broth. As with most stews or *bredies* in South Africa, the dish is named for the seasonal vegetable component most prominently featured, which in this case, is green beans. My mom and grandmother spent hours topping, tailing, and slicing buckets full of tough green beans back in the day, freezing the majority to use in green bean stew throughout winter. I go straight to the frozen aisle instead and pick up a few bags of tender haricots verts for my version of the recipe.

2 tablespoons extra-virgin olive oil

2 to 2½ pounds cross-cut beef shin (about 2 to 4 slices depending on thickness; see Note)

1 large yellow onion, finely chopped

8 large garlic cloves, minced

2 teaspoons freshly ground black pepper, plus more, if needed

1 teaspoon kosher salt

1 teaspoon ground coriander

½ teaspoon ground allspice

½ teaspoon red pepper flakes

1 fresh bay leaf

4 cups water

1 tablespoon beef stock concentrate, such as Better Than Bouillon

1 tablespoon Worcestershire sauce

1½ pounds waxy potatoes, such as Dutch yellow potatoes, quartered

2 pounds fresh or frozen haricot verts, ends trimmed

2 tablespoons unsalted butter, cubed (optional)

Grated zest and juice of 1 large lemon

Cooked rice, for serving

1   In a large (8-quart) Dutch oven, heat the oil over medium-high heat. Add the beef and cook, flipping occasionally, until browned on both sides, 4 to 5 minutes. Transfer to a plate, reserving the drippings in the pot, and reduce the heat to medium.

2   To the drippings, add the onion, garlic, black pepper, salt, coriander, allspice, red pepper flakes, and bay leaf, and cook, stirring occasionally, until the onion is soft and golden, 5 to 8 minutes. Add the browned beef, water, stock concentrate, and Worcestershire sauce. Cover and cook, stirring occasionally, until the meat is nearly tender and the liquid is reduced by half, 1 hour 45 minutes to 2 hours. Layer the potatoes on top of the beef, followed by the haricots verts, then top with the butter, if using. Continue to cook, covered, until the potatoes are fork-tender and the haricots verts are soft, 15 to 20 minutes. Remove and discard the bay leaf, then stir in the lemon juice and sprinkle with the lemon zest.

Note
Oxtails are a great alternative to the beef shin. Combine 3 pounds, joints separated, trimmed of excess fat, with enough cold water in a large bowl to cover by 1 inch, and stir in ¼ cup of distilled white vinegar. Using a serrated knife, scrape the oxtails to remove any impurities or fat. Rinse, transfer to a large plate, and pat dry with paper towels

Peppered Steak Pie

Serves 6　　Most South Africans I know are very familiar with savory, flaky, meat pies and, more than likely, quite a few of us have eaten them at ungodly hours after hanging out with friends. We call the grab-and-go hand pies "garage pies" or "petrol station pies," based on the British term for a gas station, where they are commonly sold. Each garage pie is identified by its marker, small puff pastry cutouts glued onto the tops with beaten egg before baking. I always went for the pepper steak pies because they were usually first to sell out, marked with a pastry square and filled with juicy chuck steak suspended in a thick, peppery gravy. This is my family-size version of that garage pie, with squares of puff pastry on top so that you know what you're getting.

2 tablespoons all-purpose flour, plus more for dusting

2 teaspoons kosher salt

2 teaspoons coarsely ground black pepper

1 teaspoon garlic powder

¼ teaspoon allspice

2 pounds beef chuck steak, fat trimmed, cut into 1-inch pieces

2 tablespoons extra-virgin olive oil

1 large yellow onion, chopped

4 large garlic cloves, minced

2 cups beef broth

1 cup port, dry red wine, or low-sodium beef broth

2 fresh thyme sprigs

1 sheet frozen puff pastry, thawed

1 egg, lightly beaten, for brushing

1　　Preheat the oven to 350°F with a rack in the center position.

2　　In a large bowl, combine the flour, salt, pepper, garlic powder, and allspice. Add the beef and toss until fully coated.

3　　In a large Dutch oven, heat the olive oil over medium-high heat. Once the oil just begins to smoke, working in batches, add the beef and cook, turning occasionally, until evenly browned on all sides, 1 to 2 minutes per side. Transfer the beef to a plate.

4　　Reduce the heat to medium. Add the onion and cook, stirring often, until soft and light golden brown, 6 to 8 minutes. If the bottom of the pot starts to look a little dry, add a splash of water and scrape any browned bits up with a wooden spoon. Add the garlic and cook, stirring often, until fragrant, about 1 minute.

5　　Return the beef to the pot along with any collected juices, then add the broth, port, and thyme. Increase the heat to high and bring to a boil, then cover the pot and transfer it to the oven. Cook until the meat is very tender and the sauce is thickened, 45 minutes to 1 hour. Remove from the oven and discard the thyme sprigs. Transfer the filling to an 8-inch pie dish and let cool slightly.

6　　Meanwhile, increase the oven temperature to 425°F.

7　　On a lightly floured work surface, cut the puff pastry into 3-inch squares. Brush each square with some of the egg. Arrange the puff pastry squares on top of the beef in the pot, overlapping them slightly, until the surface is covered. Bake until the pastry is puffed and golden brown, 15 to 20 minutes.

Ground Beef Bulgogi Bowls

Serves 4   With practicality at its core, these Korean-inspired beef bowls are a nod to my mom's weeknight "savory mince," ground beef browned with aromatics like onion and garlic. She seasoned the beef with whatever the pantry had to offer, sometimes a few tablespoons of brown gravy powder and water; then she bulked up the beef with any vegetables that needed to be used that week. For us that mostly meant bagged frozen vegetable mix, or potatoes, mushrooms, and peas. For many reasons, I don't do the bagged mixes anymore, replacing them with the few random vegetables in my refrigerator for this speedy dinner. I use ground beef instead of the thinly sliced rib eye that's traditional for bulgogi, and bulk up the meal with shiitake mushrooms. It's a clean-out-your-fridge kind of dinner, so feel free to swap in whichever vegetables you have available. Most nights, the urge to top the bowls with a fried egg and kimchi eaten straight from the jar at the table is too strong to resist. Any leftover bulgogi can be used to make the Bulgogi Cheesesteak Skillet Pizza (page 157).

¼ cup low-sodium soy sauce

3 tablespoons firmly packed brown sugar,
plus more to taste

2 teaspoons toasted sesame oil

1 teaspoon freshly ground black pepper

1 tablespoon avocado oil

1 medium yellow onion, finely chopped

8 ounces shiitake mushrooms,
trimmed of tough ends and thinly sliced

6 garlic cloves, minced

1 teaspoon peeled and minced fresh ginger

1 pound ground beef sirloin (90% lean/10% fat ratio,
for best results)

FOR SERVING

4 cups cooked brown rice

2 cups fresh baby spinach (or any roughly
chopped cooked vegetables, such as steamed broccoli,
roasted carrots, sautéed greens, grilled zucchini,
or stir-fried cabbage, heated)

4 large eggs, cooked to your liking

2 green onions, thinly sliced

Pickled cucumbers (page 86; optional)

Kimchi (optional)

1   In a small bowl, stir together the soy sauce, sugar, sesame oil, and pepper.

2   In a large saucepan, heat the avocado oil over medium-high heat until it just starts to shimmer. Add the onion, mushrooms, garlic, and ginger, and cook, stirring often, until the onion is translucent and the mushrooms are reduced in size, 2 to 3 minutes. Add the beef and cook, stirring occasionally, until evenly browned, 5 to 6 minutes. Pour off the excess fat, then return to the heat and stir in the soy sauce mixture. Cook, stirring occasionally, until the beef is glossy and the sauce is reduced by half, about 2 minutes.

3   TO SERVE, scoop the rice into bowls, and top with the spinach, dividing evenly. Add the beef, then top each bowl with an egg, and scatter with the green onions. Pass some pickled cucumbers and kimchi at the table, if desired.

Bulgogi Cheesesteak Skillet Pizza

Serves 6   When I taught night school students in South Korea, I frequently ate at a cafe in Wonju that I passed on the way back home. At first, the smell of sizzling bulgogi lured me in, then I started coming back for the conversations and friendship with the owners. They lived in the US for a while, so their menu reflected their passion for Korean food fused with American classics, like the loaded Philly-style cheesesteak sandwiches made with bulgogi instead of plain shaved steak. This bulgogi cheesesteak pizza takes inspiration from that sandwich, made with leftovers from the Ground Beef Bulgogi Bowls (page 154) and convenient store-bought staples.

2 tablespoons extra-virgin olive oil, divided

1 pound store-bought pizza dough, thawed, if frozen (see Notes)

1 cup jarred pizza sauce (I like Rao's)

8 ounces shredded mozzarella cheese

½ small yellow onion, thinly sliced

½ green bell pepper, thinly sliced

4 ounces cremini mushrooms, thinly sliced

1 cup beef and mushrooms from Ground Beef Bulgogi Bowls (page 154; see Notes)

½ cup shredded provolone cheese

1 green onion, green parts only, thinly sliced

1 teaspoon toasted sesame seeds

1   Preheat the oven to 450°F with a rack in the center position.

2   Brush a 12-inch cast-iron skillet with 1 tablespoon of the olive oil, coating well. Using your hands, gently stretch the dough all the way to the edges of the pan. Using a fork, poke holes evenly around the dough. Bake until the dough is pale golden, 6 to 7 minutes. Remove from the oven, and increase the oven temperature to 500°F (or as high as your oven will go).

3   Brush the remaining 1 tablespoon olive oil around the perimeter of the dough, then spread the pizza sauce evenly on top, leaving a 1-inch border around the edges. Sprinkle the mozzarella cheese evenly over the pizza sauce, followed by the onion, pepper, cremini mushrooms, beef and mushrooms, and provolone cheese.

4   Bake the pizza until the crust is golden brown and the cheese is bubbling, 6 to 8 minutes. Remove from the oven, and sprinkle with the green onion and sesame seeds.

Notes

Let your store-bought pizza dough rise to make it easier to stretch and shape. Put it in a large bowl greased with olive oil, then cover with a kitchen towel, and leave at room temperature until doubled in size, about 30 minutes.

The beef will crisp up in the oven as the pizza cooks, but if you prefer, reheat it separately and spoon it on the pizza right before serving.

No leftover bulgogi, no problem! In a pinch, I combine 8 ounces of ground beef or thinly sliced rib eye steak with ¼ cup store-bought bulgogi marinade in a skillet over medium-high heat, and cook until the beef is evenly browned and the sauce is slightly reduced and sticky, 3 to 5 minutes.

Chilled Beef Tenderloin with Tonnato Sauce

Serves 6 My South African summers were spent outside in 115-degree weather enjoying backyard cookouts with friends and family members who would trickle in the front door in a steady stream as the day progressed. My mother, attentive as she was, would hurry from the yard and usher everyone to the long table—a fold-up table laid out with platters of sliced chilled meats like gammon (smoked ham), corned beef, and pickled beef tongue with fresh salads and sauces. My mother's dedication to ensuring that everything looked great was always noticeable, and seeing everyone gush when they found such a variety on offer brought her so much joy, I could tell. I am my mother's child.

On triple-digit summer weekends here in Mississippi, I, too, offer chilled platters of meat and sauce to friends who stop by. Tenderloin is easy to slice and eat but doesn't score top points when it comes to flavor. To remedy this, I serve the slices with umami-rich Piedmontese tuna sauce, a classic accompaniment to veal in the Italian dish *vitello tonnato*. Bitter greens like watercress and radicchio balance out the meal, and add visual splendor to this easy-fancy party platter.

BEEF TENDERLOIN

1 (2-pound) beef tenderloin, trimmed of excess fat and sinew

2 teaspoons kosher salt

1 teaspoon freshly ground black pepper

2 tablespoons avocado oil

TONNATO SAUCE

½ cup mayonnaise

1 (6- to 7-ounce) jar good-quality tuna packed in olive oil (do not drain the tuna)

4 good-quality oil-packed anchovy fillets

3 tablespoons fresh lemon juice

2 tablespoons capers

1 to 2 tablespoons cold water, if needed

FOR SERVING

2 cups watercress

1 small head radicchio, leaves roughly torn

1 tablespoon capers

Extra-virgin olive oil

Flaky salt and coarsely ground black pepper

1   TO PREPARE THE BEEF, pat the tenderloin dry with paper towels. Season all over with the salt and pepper.

2   Preheat the oven to 350°F with a rack in the center position.

3   In a large cast-iron skillet, heat the avocado oil over medium-high heat. Once the oil shimmers, add the tenderloin and cook, turning frequently with tongs, until evenly browned all over, 4 to 6 minutes. Transfer the skillet to the oven, and roast until the center of the meat reaches 135°F on an instant-read thermometer for medium-rare, 15 to 18 minutes per pound—start checking the temperature of the meat after 25 minutes. Remove the tenderloin from the oven, tent with foil, and let rest for 10 minutes. The tenderloin will continue to cook as it rests. To serve the tenderloin chilled, let it cool to room temperature, then wrap it tightly in plastic wrap and refrigerate for up to 2 days.

4   MEANWHILE, TO MAKE THE TONNATO SAUCE, in a wide-mouth jar, combine the mayonnaise, tuna plus the oil it was packed in, the anchovies, lemon juice, and capers. Use an immersion blender to blend the sauce until completely smooth, adding the water to thin it out, if needed. Pour the tonnato sauce into a small serving bowl.

5   TO SERVE, slice the tenderloin and arrange on a large serving platter with the watercress and radicchio. Add the capers to the tonnato sauce, plus a glug of extra-virgin olive oil, then place the bowl on the platter. Serve, family-style, with flaky salt and coarsely ground black pepper for everyone to help themselves.

Date Night Steak
with Rosemary-Miso Butter

Serves 2   Right after my husband's first deployment to Kuwait ended, we got married and moved into a small apartment in El Paso, Texas, to begin our new life. For a whole year prior, I had waited for DJ while I taught in South Korea, where we first met. It was such a relief to step off the airplane in America and see him for the first time in so long, and in good health.

The first meal I cooked in our new apartment was a buttery steak. I knew that he missed eating the food that we enjoyed together while we were still dating. Unfortunately, my nervousness as a new wife combined with jet lag caused me to oversalt the steak, but he still ate it as if it were his last meal on earth. That's love!

Since then, we've made it a tradition to spend Wednesday nights at home, sharing a good quality steak slathered in butter on date night. It's especially delicious with rosemary-miso butter, which adds a special savory touch to the juicy seared steak as it cascades down, pooling onto the plate to mingle with our favorite sides. It's roasted potatoes or crispy fries for me, seasoned with truffle salt to complement the earthiness of the miso in the butter.

1 (1-pound) rib eye or New York strip steak,
about 1 inch thick

1 teaspoon kosher salt

1 teaspoon freshly ground black pepper

1 tablespoon avocado oil

Rosemary-Miso Butter (recipe follows), for serving

Triple Truffle-Roasted Fingerling Potatoes (page 229),
or frozen fries cooked according to the package directions
and sprinkled with truffle salt (optional)

1   Season the steak on both sides with the salt and pepper. Let it sit, uncovered, at room temperature for 30 minutes.

2   In a large cast-iron skillet, heat the oil over medium-high heat. When the oil just starts to smoke, add the steak and cook until the internal temperature reaches 135°F on an instant-read thermometer for medium-rare, about 5 minutes per side. Using tongs, turn the steak onto its edge (where the fat cap is), and hold it there to cook until the fat is crispy, 1 to 2 minutes. Transfer the steak to a platter, and top with the rosemary-miso butter. Let the steak rest for at least 5 minutes while the butter melts and forms a dipping pool around it, then slice against the grain (see Note) before serving with the potatoes.

Note
To slice against the grain, find the long strands or muscle fibers that run parallel in the meat, then slice perpendicular to them. Shortening the long strands leads to less chewy meat, juicier bites, and easier eating! This is an essential technique when it comes to any cut of meat, but a good steak is an investment that you're definitely going to want to enjoy at its best.

ROSEMARY-MISO BUTTER

2 tablespoons unsalted butter, softened

1 teaspoon white miso

1 teaspoon finely chopped fresh rosemary needles

In a small bowl, combine the butter, miso, and rosemary. Mix until all the ingredients are evenly incorporated.

five

PORK
&
LAMB

Halmoni's Soft Tofu, Bacon & Kimchi Soup (Kimchi Jjigae)

Serves 4 In my third year as an English teacher in South Korea, I started tutoring on the side and received an interview request from Dr. and Mrs. Kim, parents of Joo Ha (who goes by the English name Oprah) and Dong Ha (who goes by Flora). The interview was brief, but the busy couple hired me on the spot, and for four years, I spent Monday and Wednesday evenings teaching their daughters English at the Kim family home. The girls were remarkable, and so was their *halmoni* (grandmother), who, without fail, cooked dinner for us to have all together once Dr. and Mrs. Kim got home from work.

Halmoni wasn't a woman of many words, but she showed her dedication to the family in an unspoken manner: the meticulous way she peeled and sliced fruit for everyone, to make a pretty plate for her perfectly set table, was a pure act of love. In the summer, those plates included bite-size pieces of Korean melon (*chamoe*), segmented Jeju Island tangerines (*hallabong*) from which she painstakingly removed all the pith and membranes; and in the fall, Korean pear (*bae*) or Fuji apples that she peeled with such delicate precision the long spiral of skin never broke. She executed her unassuming role to keep the family going gracefully and served them with humility. That was incredibly inspirational and reminded me of my mother and grandmother in South Africa. During those years, she was my halmoni, too, and the Kims became my de facto family almost 7,000 miles away from "home." I'm forever thankful for their hospitality, and the way they made me feel like a valued member of their family, not just a tutor.

One of my favorite meals Halmoni made was *kimchi jjigae*. I first ate this pork and aged kimchi soup at their dinner table, but it wasn't until later I found out how to make it. Halmoni quickly explained the steps during our drive to the airport when I flew away to marry DJ in America. I continue to cook my version here in Mississippi when I miss my other "home," serving fruit for dessert, prepped and peeled for my loved ones. Dear Kim family, thank you for everything.

4 slices uncured thick-cut bacon (each ¼ inch thick), roughly chopped

4 ounces oyster or shiitake mushrooms, sliced

6 large garlic cloves, minced

2 teaspoons peeled and minced fresh ginger

1½ cups chopped aged kimchi (undrained; see Notes on page 180)

1 tablespoon mild gochujang

1 tablespoon firmly packed light brown sugar

6 cups Chicken Stock (page 259) or low-sodium chicken broth

2 tablespoons soy sauce, plus more to taste

10 ounces baby bok choy, leaves separated

1 (12-ounce) package soft tofu, drained

FOR SERVING

Pasteurized egg yolks (optional)

Toasted sesame oil

Toasted sesame seeds

Cooked short-grain rice

1 In a large (5-quart) saucepan over medium heat, place the bacon and mushrooms, and cook, stirring often, until the bacon fat is rendered and the mushrooms are slightly caramelized around the edges, about 5 minutes. Drain all but 2 tablespoons of the fat from the saucepan. Add the garlic and ginger, and cook, stirring occasionally, until fragrant, about 2 minutes. Add the kimchi, gochujang, and sugar, and cook, scraping any brown bits off the bottom of the saucepan with a wooden spoon, 3 to 5 minutes. Pour in the stock and soy sauce, bring to a simmer and cook, uncovered, for 10 minutes, adding the bok choy and large spoonfuls of the tofu halfway through. Once the tofu is hot, the soup is ready to be served.

2 Divide the soup among bowls. If using egg yolks, drop one into each bowl, letting the piping-hot broth cook it gently. Drizzle each bowl with about ½ teaspoon of sesame oil and sprinkle with sesame seeds. Serve with rice.

Late Summer Sausage Supper

Serves 4 There are a few confusing weeks between the end of summer and the beginning of fall when peaches and cherry tomatoes are really at their best, but the cooler nights call for something hearty and satisfying. That's when I love to make this easy, delicious supper with savory sausages, sweet peaches, cherry tomatoes, and creamy Parmesan spaghetti squash. It's endlessly adaptable and feels cozy without being too heavy. Switch it up as the seasons change, letting what's available at your local market guide you.

1 large spaghetti squash (about 4 pounds)

2 tablespoons extra-virgin olive oil

1½ pounds sweet Italian sausage

¼ cup dry white wine, such as Chardonnay

2 large yellow peaches, sliced into 1-inch wedges

2 cups cherry tomatoes

1 small red onion, cut into ¼-inch wedges

1 small serrano chili, seeded and thinly sliced (optional)

1 teaspoon freshly ground black pepper

½ teaspoon flaky salt

1 cup freshly grated Parmesan cheese

4 tablespoons salted butter

6 to 8 fresh basil leaves, torn

1 fresh oregano sprig, leaves stripped

1 Preheat the oven to 400°F with a rack in the center position.

2 Microwave the whole spaghetti squash on high power for 5 minutes. This softens the rind for easier cutting. Use a serrated bread knife to cut the squash in half lengthwise, then scoop out the seeds with a spoon and discard. Place the squash on a rimmed sheet pan, cut side down, and roast until very tender, 50 minutes to 1 hour. Set aside to cool.

3 Meanwhile, reduce the oven temperature to 375°F.

4 In a large skillet, heat the oil over medium heat. Once the oil shimmers, add the sausage and cook, turning halfway through, until light golden brown on both sides, about 2 minutes per side. Add the wine, then arrange the peaches, tomatoes, red onion, and serrano chili, if using, evenly around the sausages, and sprinkle with the pepper and salt. Roast in the oven until the sausage is golden brown, sizzling, and fully cooked through, 18 to 20 minutes.

5 Meanwhile, into a food processor, scoop the slightly cooled squash flesh and add the Parmesan and butter. Pulse until the squash is creamy and the butter is melted, 1 to 2 minutes.

6 Divide the spaghetti squash among plates and top with the roasted sausage, peaches, and tomatoes. Sprinkle with the basil and oregano leaves.

Oven-Baked Gochujang Ribs
(Ribs for the Table)

Serves 6 to 8 Occasionally, when friends visit, I make a big platter of sticky ribs for the table for everyone to gnaw on while chit-chatting, the same way we enjoy ribs with family in South Africa.

While reminiscing about the past, I tried to re-create a South African barbecue sauce known as monkeygland sauce, but couldn't quite commit to the cooked tomato and wine-based concoction. (Don't worry, it's just a name—there's no actual monkey in the sauce.) To be frank, it's my mom's favorite but also a relic from the eighties where I think it should stay. It was freeing to admit that my tastes have changed, and I decided to baste the ribs with the Korean flavors that I enjoy now. Everyday Gochujang Sauce (page 259) is a mainstay in my kitchen and makes an easy no-cook glaze for baby back ribs. The maple syrup in the sauce caramelizes nicely under the broiler, much to everyone's delight. Two smaller racks work best here; not only do they cook faster, but they are also easier to pick up and eat without looking like you belong in medieval times.

2 racks baby back ribs (about 2 pounds each)

2 teaspoons kosher salt

1½ teaspoons freshly ground black pepper

1 teaspoon garlic powder

1 cup apple cider, low-sodium chicken broth, or water

½ cup Everyday Gochujang Sauce (page 259)

1   Preheat the oven to 325°F with a rack in the center position.

2   Set a wire rack on a rimmed sheet pan. Place the ribs on top, and pat both sides of each rack very dry with paper towels. Carefully peel away the thin membrane attached to the underside of the ribs and discard. Season the ribs all over with the salt, pepper, and garlic powder.

3   Carefully pour the apple cider into the sheet pan, and wrap everything tightly with heavy-duty aluminum foil. Bake until the ribs are very tender and the thickest part of the meat away from the bone reaches 195°F on an instant-read thermometer, 1 hour 30 minutes to 2 hours.

4   Carefully remove the sheet pan from the oven, lift off the wire rack, and pour off any remaining liquid. Line the sheet pan with aluminum foil, and place the rack with the ribs on top.

5   Set the oven to broil.

6   Using a silicone brush, baste the ribs on both sides with the gochujang sauce. Broil until the sauce is glossy and the ribs are sticky, about 5 minutes per side. Repeat once more and serve.

Pork Schnitzel with Pickled Persimmon Salad

Serves 4 The schnitzel of my childhood was draped with a slice of processed American cheese and a rich mushroom sauce. It was a specialty at the local steak house, served with crispy onion rings and fries. We usually polished off our meal with a "Chico the Clown" dessert, a rather scary-looking scoop of vanilla ice cream with an upside-down cone hat and droopy Skittles eyes as the dye from the candy ran down the melted ice cream face. *Shudders in horror.* While I'd probably pass on Chico now, I still love a good cheesy schnitzel. Using potato flakes combined with Parmesan instead of bread crumbs to coat the pork gives the thinly pounded chops lots of crunch and umami-rich flavor while also keeping things gluten free, if you need them to be. The persimmon salad gives the crispy fried pork some acidity, taking it to fall without the heaviness. Swap out the persimmons for pears or apples, and if blue cheese isn't your thing, try goat cheese or shaved Parmesan instead.

SALAD

2 medium Fuyu persimmons, cut into ½-inch wedges

1 small shallot, finely chopped

2 tablespoons apple cider vinegar

1 tablespoon pure maple syrup

¼ teaspoon kosher salt

¼ teaspoon freshly ground black pepper

4 cups baby kale

½ small head radicchio, leaves roughly torn

½ cup roughly chopped toasted pecans

¼ cup crumbled blue cheese (optional; I like the creaminess of Saint Agur)

SCHNITZEL

2 large eggs

1 tablespoon stone-ground mustard

¾ cup dried potato flakes (or panko bread crumbs, if gluten is not an issue)

½ cup freshly grated Parmesan or Pecorino Romano cheese

½ teaspoon fresh thyme leaves

½ teaspoon finely chopped fresh sage leaves

4 (4-ounce) boneless pork chops, pounded ¼ inch thick

1 teaspoon kosher salt

½ teaspoon freshly ground black pepper

¼ cup extra-virgin olive oil

2 tablespoons unsalted butter

Flaky salt

1 TO START THE SALAD, in a large serving bowl, combine the persimmons with the shallot, vinegar, maple syrup, salt, and pepper, and toss until well coated. Let sit for 10 minutes at room temperature for the flavors to meld.

2 MEANWHILE, TO MAKE THE SCHNITZEL, in a shallow bowl, whisk together the eggs and mustard until completely smooth. In another shallow bowl, stir together the potato flakes, Parmesan, thyme, and sage.

3 Season both sides of the pork chops with the salt and pepper. Dip each chop in the eggs, and flip until evenly coated on both sides. Press each chop into the potato flake mixture, flipping, until both sides are well coated.

4 In a large skillet, heat the oil and butter over medium heat. Once the butter is melted, add the pork and cook until golden brown and crisp, 2 to 3 minutes per side. Transfer to a paper towel–lined plate and sprinkle with flaky salt.

5 TO FINISH THE SALAD, to the bowl with the persimmons, add the kale, radicchio, pecans, and blue cheese, if using. Toss and serve with the schnitzel.

Miso-Braised Pork Shoulder

Serves 6 to 8   There's something about having a large hunk of cooked meat on standby for use in a multitude of meals that really gets me going. While I didn't grow up eating pork (we had an incident with a suckling pig, don't ask), I ate my fair share in South Korea. There, I discovered that most pork dishes are greatly improved with umami-laden soybean pastes like *doènjang* and miso. Here, miso adds depth and subtle flavor to enhance rather than overpower.

The onions in this savory braise are probably my favorite part of the meal because they take on the flavor of mellowed-down apple cider vinegar. One thing is for certain, you're going to want to have some left over for the Miso Pulled Pork Nachos (page 63). Set it aside before anyone gets to the pork, or else it might disappear right before your eyes.

1 (4-pound) bone-in pork shoulder

1 tablespoon kosher salt

1 tablespoon coarsely ground black pepper

8 large garlic cloves, thinly sliced, divided

3 tablespoons salted butter

2 large yellow onions, halved and sliced

1 cup Chicken Stock (page 259) or low-sodium chicken broth

1 cup unfiltered apple juice, pear juice, or apple cider

½ cup apple cider vinegar

¼ cup white miso

2 tablespoons pure maple syrup

2 fresh thyme sprigs

1   Preheat the oven to 350°F with a rack in the lower third position.

2   Using a sharp paring knife, cut 8 to 10 (½-inch) slits in the fat cap of the pork shoulder, and season all over with the salt and pepper. Stuff about one-quarter of the garlic slices into the slits. Cover and refrigerate for at least 3 hours, and up to overnight. Remove the pork from the refrigerator 1 hour before cooking.

3   In a large Dutch oven over medium-high heat, combine the butter, onions, and remaining garlic, and cook, stirring occasionally, until the onions just start to soften, 5 to 6 minutes. Add the chicken stock, apple juice, vinegar, miso, maple syrup, and thyme sprigs, and cook, stirring, until the miso dissolves. Nestle in the pork shoulder, skin side up, cover, and transfer to the oven. Cook until the pork is fork-tender, the liquid is reduced, and the onions are golden brown and caramelized, 2½ to 3 hours. Remove the pot from the oven.

4   Increase the oven temperature to 400°F.

5   Uncover the pot and return to the oven. Cook until the pork is golden brown on top, about 15 minutes more. Let rest for 10 minutes, then discard the thyme stems. Pull off pieces of the pork with tongs, stir into the braised onion gravy, and serve.

Potato Soup with Smoked Sausage & Greens

Serves 4   Inspired by the Portuguese soup *caldo verde*, but with a Southern twist, this flavorful family favorite is delicious any time of year. I use andouille or smoked beef sausage instead of traditional Portuguese *chouriço*, a generous amount of smoked paprika, and any greens depending on what I can find. Before the local grocery store around the corner, Piggly Wiggly, closed, I used the freshest Mississippi-grown turnip or mustard greens. Then it became collard greens, chard, or trusty kale that was easier to find elsewhere. The beauty of this soup lies in its simplicity and adaptability, so use what you have, and swap out the potatoes for sweet potatoes, cubed pumpkin, or even cauliflower for a lower-carb option, if desired.

2 teaspoons extra-virgin olive oil

1 pound andouille or smoked beef sausage, sliced into ⅛-inch-thick coins

1 large yellow onion, finely chopped

½ red bell pepper, finely chopped

2 tablespoons minced garlic

2 pounds russet potatoes, peeled and cut into 1-inch cubes

1 tablespoon smoked paprika (see Note)

1 teaspoon Cajun seasoning

6 cups Chicken Stock (page 259) or low-sodium chicken broth

4 cups roughly chopped leafy greens, such as mustard or turnip greens, kale, collards, or chard

2 tablespoons heavy whipping cream (optional)

Kosher salt and freshly ground black pepper, as needed

In a large Dutch oven, heat the oil over medium heat. Add the sausage and cook, stirring occasionally, until the edges are slightly caramelized and the fat is partially rendered, about 5 minutes. Add the onion, bell pepper, and garlic, and cook, stirring occasionally, until the onion is translucent and the garlic is fragrant, 5 to 8 minutes. Add the potatoes, smoked paprika, Cajun seasoning, and chicken stock, and cook, covered, until the potatoes are very tender, almost breaking apart, 20 to 25 minutes. Stir in the greens and heavy cream, if using, and cook, covered, until the greens are wilted, about 2 minutes. Taste the soup and season with salt and pepper, if needed.

Note

Use quality Spanish paprika that smells very fragrant for best results. I like deeply smoky Spanish paprika (pimenton) from Penzey's, The Spice House, or Spice Tribe.

Crispy Grilled Lamb Chops with Fresh Chakalaka Salad

Serves 2   I've always loved the smell of crispy lamb chops and their drippings as they hit the hot embers of our grill. We South Africans prefer to cook our lamb chops a little longer, typically set over the hot coals of a live fire. This ensures the crispy fat cap, which in my opinion is the best part of it all. When I can, a wood fire is still my preferred method because the smoke imparts great flavor. If you're able to, I highly recommend it; however, the stovetop method that I use on a more regular basis renders delicious results in its own right.

However you decide to cook them, the lamb chops are one of the main components of a very specific weekend cookout or braai plate in South Africa. If you visit the motherland and eat meat cooked over the fire, chances are it'll be served alongside potato salad, *braaibroodjies* (see page 219), and a spicy stewed cabbage and pepper relish known as *chakalaka*. Isn't it fun to say? My American friends and family always get a kick out of trying to pronounce it at parties when we grill in the summer. To spend less time cooking inside and move away from heavier sides, I serve my crispy grilled lamb chops with a fresh, no-cook take on chakalaka that's more like a salad (and ready to go in minutes). I use tender napa cabbage instead of the usual green cabbage, and the pickling liquid from jarred cherry peppers to season the vegetables. The chakalaka is easy to customize with add-ins like chickpeas, beans, or grains, and leftovers can be used to perk up sandwiches, eggs, or even tacos.

LAMB CHOPS

3 tablespoons extra-virgin olive oil

2 tablespoons balsamic vinegar

2 teaspoons coriander seeds, coarsely ground

2 teaspoons kosher salt

2 teaspoons freshly ground black pepper

1½ teaspoons smoked paprika

1 teaspoon garlic powder

2 pounds untrimmed lamb chops (about eight 1-inch-thick chops from 1 rack)

CHAKALAKA SALAD

2 cups finely shredded napa cabbage

¼ red bell pepper, thinly sliced

¼ yellow bell pepper, thinly sliced

¼ green bell pepper, thinly sliced

¼ small red onion, thinly sliced

¼ cup sliced pickled cherry peppers, drained, plus 2 tablespoons of the pickling liquid

2 tablespoons extra-virgin olive oil

2 tablespoons roughly chopped fresh cilantro leaves

1   MAKE THE MARINADE FOR THE LAMB: In a large bowl, whisk together the olive oil, vinegar, coriander seeds, salt, pepper, smoked paprika, and garlic powder until well combined. Add the lamb chops and gently toss to coat, then let sit at room temperature for 15 minutes.

2   MEANWHILE, MAKE THE SALAD: In a large serving bowl, toss together the cabbage, bell peppers, onion, cherry peppers, pickling liquid, olive oil, and cilantro until combined and the vegetables are well coated.

3   Heat a large cast-iron skillet or grill pan over medium-high heat (open a window or a door and turn on the vent hood, if possible). Once hot, add the lamb chops in batches and cook, undisturbed, until visible char marks appear on the bottom and the fat around the edges is deep golden brown, 4 to 5 minutes. Flip and cook on the other side to your desired doneness (135°F for medium), 3 to 4 minutes. Using tongs, hold one lamb chop at a time on its edge (where the fat cap is), and cook until the fat is crispy, 1 to 2 minutes. Transfer to a platter and serve with the salad.

Kimchi-Braised Lamb Shanks

Serves 4 Here's my interpretation of the oven-braised lamb legs that I ate as a kid, but with more readily available lamb shanks, and aged, well-fermented kimchi for an unexpected, funky twist. Upon first impression they might seem like an odd couple, and you wouldn't typically find lamb in Korean cuisine, but the robust, grassy qualities of this meat actually agree with assertive foods like kimchi. If you think about it, lamb and anchovies are a proven pairing, and kimchi contains fish sauce or salted shrimp, which have a similar flavor profile to anchovies, so it's a distant cousin kind of match. Braising the two in the oven marries them, and when you spoon the caramelized, velvety braised kimchi over these meltingly tender, sweet lamb shanks, you'll know what I mean. Honestly, I'm hoping that lamb and kimchi will one day become a proven pairing, too.

Any leftover lamb can be pulled off the bone, combined with the braised kimchi, and used to make the most delicious kimchi grilled cheese (see page 180) ever as a midnight snack.

4 large lamb shanks (4 to 5 pounds total; see Notes)

2 teaspoons kosher salt, plus more if needed (see Notes)

2 teaspoons freshly ground black pepper

2 tablespoons extra-virgin olive oil

1 large yellow onion, chopped

2 cups chopped homemade (see page 260) or store-bought kimchi, preferably aged and well-fermented (see Notes)

8 garlic cloves, finely minced

1 tablespoon peeled and minced fresh ginger

1½ tablespoons sugar

12 medium carrots, scrubbed and halved crosswise or cut into 3-inch-long pieces

2½ cups Chicken Stock (page 259) or low-sodium chicken broth

2 fresh rosemary sprigs

2 green onions, thinly sliced at an angle, for garnish

Cooked rice, polenta, or your favorite green vegetables, for serving

1 In a large bowl or on a rimmed sheet pan, season the lamb shanks with the salt and pepper and let sit, covered, at room temperature for 1 to 2 hours before cooking. The lamb shanks can also be seasoned in advance and refrigerated, covered, for up to 24 hours. Remove from the refrigerator 1 hour before cooking.

2 Preheat the oven to 350°F with a rack in the center position.

3 In a large Dutch oven, heat the oil over medium-high heat. Working in two batches, add the shanks and sear, turning often with tongs, until as evenly golden brown as possible all over, 3 to 5 minutes per side. Transfer to a plate, reserving the drippings in the pot. (Pour off all but 2 tablespoons of the drippings if your lamb is particularly fatty.)

4 To the reserved drippings, add the onion, and cook over medium heat, stirring occasionally, until light golden and softened, about 5 minutes. If the pot becomes too dry, add a splash of water and scrape any browned bits off the bottom with a wooden spoon. Add the kimchi, garlic, ginger, and sugar, and cook, stirring occasionally, until some of the kimchi is slightly caramelized around the edges, 8 to 10 minutes. Return the lamb shanks to the pot, nestling them into the vegetables so that they are as level as possible. Arrange the carrots on top, pour over the chicken stock, then add the rosemary sprigs. Cover the Dutch oven with the lid.

5 Transfer to the oven and cook until the meat is very tender and the stock is reduced by half, 2 to 2½ hours. Taste and adjust the salt, if needed.

6 Transfer the lamb shanks to a serving bowl, and spoon over the braised kimchi, carrots, and reduced sauce. Sprinkle with the green onions and put it on the table, family-style, with individual bowls of cooked rice, polenta, or your favorite green vegetables.

continues

Notes

I absolutely adore American lamb and find it to be high in flavor, and much less gamey than imported lamb from Australia. I highly recommend using it for this recipe, and since these shanks are larger, you'll need to pull out your biggest Dutch oven so they're submerged in the liquid. Alternatively, transfer the shanks to a large, deep roasting pan and cover tightly with aluminum foil to lock in the steam before finishing them in the oven.

Salt levels in kimchi vary greatly, so taste your kimchi before seasoning the lamb, and add less salt in the beginning. You can always add more at the end.

Aged, well-fermented kimchi is deeper in color, and the cabbage leaves are almost translucent, tender, with not much crunch. The aroma is stronger. Oftentimes, I use kimchi that is at least 3 months old. To age kimchi, leave the container at room temperature for a week, ensuring that the cabbage is submerged in liquid, so it will not spoil, only ferment. I sometimes use a canning weight or sterilized small heavy bowl to make sure the kimchi stays submerged.

LATE-NIGHT GRILLED CHEESE
WITH KIMCHI-BRAISED LAMB

Serves 1

½ cup shredded sharp Cheddar cheese

½ cup Kimchi-Braised LambShanks (including kimchi and meat pulled from bones)

2 slices whole-grain sourdough bread

1 tablespoon unsalted butter, divided

½ teaspoon unhulled sesame seeds (optional)

1   Sandwich the cheese and kimchi braised lamb between the bread.

2   In a small nonstick skillet, melt half of the butter over medium heat. Once the butter stops bubbling and smells nutty, add the sandwich, and cover with a lid. Cook until the cheese is melting around the edges of the bread, 2 to 3 minutes. Remove the lid and lift the sandwich with a spatula. Add the remaining butter to the skillet, swirling to coat, until melted. Flip the sandwich and cook, uncovered, for another 2 minutes. Transfer the sandwich to a plate, and sprinkle with the sesame seeds.

Spicy Pork & Eggplant Lettuce Wraps

Serves 4 to 6   The inspiration for this recipe came from spicy *samgyupsal*, sizzling slices of pork belly, that I love to cook over the hot charcoal grills at my favorite Korean barbecue restaurants in Atlanta. The caramelized pork belly is typically served with a multitude of side dishes or *banchan*, which, when combined with the pork in a lettuce wrap, creates a symphony of complementary flavors. My at-home interpretation has similar flavors, but instead of pork belly, I use quick-cooking ground pork that's a little easier to find at the local Piggly Wiggly. I add eggplant, and sometimes king oyster mushrooms, and serve the fragrant pork family-style, with a tangy cabbage slaw, fresh sliced cucumbers, lettuce, and perilla leaves for wrapping. The Miso Tahini Sauce (page 262), is my version of the classic Korean condiment for grilled meats, *ssamjang*, which really brings the whole wrap together. Try not to skip it!

CABBAGE SLAW
4 cups finely shredded red cabbage

4 green onions, chopped

2 tablespoons fresh lime juice

1 teaspoon toasted sesame seeds

½ teaspoon kosher salt

PORK AND EGGPLANT
2 tablespoons avocado oil

1 small white onion, finely chopped

1 pound ground pork (see Note)

1 small eggplant (about 8 ounces), diced into ½-inch cubes

6 garlic cloves, minced

1 tablespoon honey

1 tablespoon mirin or soju

2 teaspoons peeled and minced fresh ginger

2 teaspoons gochugaru

2 teaspoons soy sauce

1 teaspoon toasted sesame oil

FOR SERVING
2 heads butter lettuce, leaves separated

Perilla leaves (optional)

2 Persian cucumbers, thinly sliced

Miso Tahini Sauce (page 262) or ssamjang

1   TO MAKE THE CABBAGE SLAW, in a medium serving bowl, toss together the cabbage, green onions, lime juice, sesame seeds, and salt until well combined. Cover and refrigerate until ready to serve.

2   TO COOK THE PORK AND EGGPLANT, in a large wok or cast-iron skillet, heat the avocado oil over medium-high heat. Once the oil shimmers, add the onion and cook, stirring occasionally, until light golden brown, 1 to 2 minutes. Add the pork, eggplant, garlic, honey, mirin, ginger, gochugaru, soy sauce, and sesame oil, and cook, breaking up any large clumps of pork and stirring occasionally, until the pork and eggplant are browned and slightly crisp in places, 4 to 5 minutes.

3   TO SERVE, transfer the pork and eggplant to a bowl, and serve family-style with the cabbage slaw, letting everyone assemble wraps with the lettuce, perilla leaves, if using, cucumbers, and miso tahini sauce.

Note
Instead of ground pork, you can substitute ground turkey, boneless skinless chicken thighs cut into 1-inch pieces, or thinly sliced rib eye steak or pork sirloin.

Lamb Meatballs for a Mezze Platter

Serves 4   There's something so laissez-faire about gathering the foods you love, then arranging everything beautifully on a board to place in front of people. The variety of flavors, textures, and colors alone is appetizing, and there's bound to be something for everyone.

I grew up eating this way at least once a week on plates that Mom described as "*los kos*" (loose food)—piecemeal configurations of pan-fried lamb meatballs served with bits and bobs from the refrigerator. Some days that included a chopped tomato, cucumber, and olive salad with leftover rice; other days, boiled potatoes or corn on the cob. The meals were relatively easy to cobble together, so my sisters and I became sous chefs, learning the value of curbing waste in the process.

Here in Mississippi, I apply the principle of eating "los kos" as often as possible using a semi-homemade approach for casual dinners. They center around oven-baked lamb meatballs, supplemented with my favorite Mediterranean refrigerator and pantry staples. Stores like Trader Joe's are constantly stocking their shelves with interesting prepared foods to add. My haul almost always includes marinated olives or peppers from the deli, and I serve it all on a big board with the meatballs alongside, mezze-style.

MEATBALLS
1 pound ground lamb or beef

1 small yellow onion, finely chopped

4 garlic cloves, minced

¼ cup chopped fresh parsley

1 tablespoon chopped fresh oregano leaves

1 tablespoon Dijon mustard

1 teaspoon grated lemon zest

1 teaspoon kosher salt

½ teaspoon freshly cracked black pepper

MEZZE (OPTIONAL)
2 Persian cucumbers, sliced

Cherry tomatoes on the vine

Dolmades

Pepperoncini, Peppadew, or roasted bell peppers

Toasted pita bread

Hummus

½ cup olives

½ cup Yogurt Feta Sauce (page 263) or tzatziki

Extra-virgin olive oil, for drizzling

¼ cup loosely packed fresh herbs such as mint and dill sprigs, for garnish

1   MAKE THE MEATBALLS: Preheat the oven to 375°F with a rack in the center position. Line a rimmed sheet pan with aluminum foil.

2   In a large bowl, gently stir together the lamb, onion, garlic, parsley, oregano, Dijon, lemon zest, salt, and pepper until evenly combined. Form into 1-ounce meatballs (about the size of a Ping-Pong ball), gently rolling each one in your palms, then transfer to the prepared sheet pan as you go. Roast in the oven until the meatballs are just cooked through and evenly browned, 13 to 15 minutes.

3   MEANWHILE, PREPARE THE MEZZE, IF DESIRED: Arrange the cucumbers, tomatoes, dolmades, pepperoncini, and pita bread on a large serving board. Spoon the hummus, olives, and feta sauce into small individual serving bowls, then drizzle with olive oil and place on the board. Once the meatballs are cooked, arrange them directly on the board. Or feel free to get creative and arrange your components on a platter however you like! Garnish with the herbs and serve.

Lamb Sosaties
with Apricots, Bay & Onion

Serves 4   On Sundays in South Africa, you can smell these curried lamb skewers cooking over live fires throughout every neighborhood as families gather around the braai, an Afrikaans word that describes both the social event and the actual technique of grilling over a live fire. These sweet and savory skewers can be made with pork, beef, or lamb and are displayed in almost every South African butcher's counter or grocery store, already prepped and marinated for convenience. Stateside, I make my own *sosaties* with boneless lamb and marinate them overnight when time permits. We love serving these to guests who visit our home for a braai, with a round of Springbokkie (a traditional peppermint liqueur shot; see page 45)—the best conversation starter!

¼ cup avocado or canola oil

¼ cup red wine vinegar

¼ cup port or dry sherry

2 tablespoons apricot jam or preserves, or District Six Apricot Chutney (page 263)

1 tablespoon Worcestershire sauce

1 tablespoon mild curry powder

2 teaspoons ground coriander

2 teaspoons cornstarch

2 teaspoons kosher salt

1 teaspoon freshly ground black pepper

2 pounds lamb from a boneless leg, cut into 1-inch cubes (ask your butcher for kebab meat)

1 large red onion, cut into 1-inch cubes

2 cups dried apricot halves

1 fresh bay leaf, plus 12 more for skewering

1   In a large bowl, whisk together the avocado oil, vinegar, port, jam, Worcestershire sauce, curry powder, coriander, cornstarch, salt, and pepper until well combined. Add the lamb, onion, dried apricots, and 1 bay leaf, and gently toss to combine until the meat is fully coated. Cover and refrigerate for at least 3 hours, preferably overnight.

2   Thread the lamb, onion, apricots, and remaining bay leaves onto metal skewers, alternating between each ingredient until nothing remains.

3   Heat a grill or large grill pan to medium heat. Grill the skewers, turning occasionally, until the edges are lightly charred and the meat is golden or caramelized, about 4 minutes per side. Serve warm.

six

EGGS

Shebashuka

Serves 4   Depending on who you ask, the chunky onion and tomato relish that these eggs are poached in is known as *sheba*, *smoor*, or *sous* in South Africa. It's typically eaten as a side with maize porridge and grilled meats and sausage. Every family has their own version, ranging from a very simple combination of fresh tomatoes stewed with onions to more complex recipes that include chili, herbs, and spices. When money was tight, my mother would get creative and spin her sheba into a full meal by adding sliced hot dog coins and more sugar than was necessary as a way to entice us kids to finish our dinner. Those leftovers made a fine breakfast with baked eggs and buttered white bread the next morning. We never felt deprived, and regardless of circumstance, I continue to make these humble dishes for my loved ones today.

Inspired by my mom's improvised breakfast, I poach eggs in the sheba sauce, in the style of *shakshuka*—adding smoked sausage and a hint of ginger but not all her spoonfuls of sugar. If you want to bulk up the meal even more, add any sliced mushrooms or roughly chopped greens when cooking the onions, then continue with the recipe as directed.

SHEBA

2 tablespoons extra-virgin olive oil

8 ounces smoked sausage, halved lengthwise, then sliced into ¼-inch-thick half-moons (omit if making sheba for the Farmer's Sausage, Egg & Cheese Sandwiches on page 192)

1 small red onion, chopped

4 large garlic cloves, minced

1 teaspoon peeled and minced fresh ginger

1 teaspoon kosher salt

½ teaspoon freshly ground black pepper

½ teaspoon ground coriander

½ teaspoon dried oregano

½ cup dry white wine, such as Sauvignon Blanc, or water

1 (14-ounce) can cherry tomatoes

1 cup halved cherry tomatoes

1½ tablespoons sugar

1 tablespoon Worcestershire sauce

SHUKA

4 large eggs

Roughly chopped fresh oregano leaves, for garnish

4 slices bread, toasted and buttered, for serving

1   MAKE THE SHEBA: In a large saucepan, heat the oil over medium heat. Add the sausage and cook, stirring occasionally, until lightly browned and crisp around the edges, 2 to 3 minutes. Add the onion, garlic, ginger, salt, pepper, coriander, and dried oregano, and cook, stirring occasionally, until the onion just starts to soften and the spices are fragrant, about 3 minutes. Stir in the white wine, canned and fresh tomatoes, sugar, and Worcestershire sauce; cover and cook, stirring occasionally, until the flavors have melded and the sauce is thickened slightly, 8 to 10 minutes.

2   MAKE THE SHUKA: Reduce the heat to medium-low. Use the back of a ladle or spoon to make four wells in the tomato mixture. Crack the eggs, one at a time, into a small bowl, then gently transfer each egg into a well, taking care not to break the yolks. Cover and cook until the whites are set and the yolks still jiggle slightly, 5 to 8 minutes. Garnish with the chopped oregano leaves and serve with the bread.

Farmer's Sausage Patties

Serves 8 (see Note)   Widely considered to be one of South Africa's national foods, *boerewors* is a coiled beef and pork sausage that translates to "farmer's sausage" in English. The sausage is found everywhere in South Africa, but buying it from suppliers here in the US gets pricey. When I have a hankering for boerewors now, I make these patties with easy-to-find beer brats and ground beef. I season the meat with coriander, cloves, and nutmeg just like traditional boerewors—but I can cook the sausage quickly in a skillet instead of having to stuff anything into a casing. Yeah, definitely not happening.

Use the patties in the Farmer's Sausage, Egg & Cheese Sandwiches (page 192) or serve them with Herby Horseradish Mashed Potatoes (see page 139) and Sheba (see page 188).

1 pound ground beef chuck or sirloin

4 (3.5-ounce) beer brats, casings removed and discarded

1 large egg

½ cup panko bread crumbs

¼ cup distilled white vinegar

¼ cup cold water

1 tablespoon coriander seeds, coarsely ground

1 teaspoon freshly ground black pepper

¾ teaspoon kosher salt

½ teaspoon ground cloves

¼ teaspoon freshly grated nutmeg

2 tablespoons extra-virgin olive oil, divided

1   In a large bowl, combine the ground beef, brats, egg, panko, vinegar, water, coriander, pepper, salt, cloves, and nutmeg. Gently knead until well incorporated. Cover and refrigerate for at least 30 minutes, preferably 1 hour, and up to overnight before forming the sausage patties.

2   Using your hands, form the sausage mixture into eight (4-ounce) patties, about ½ inch thick and 4 inches wide.

3   In a large skillet, heat 1 tablespoon of the oil over medium heat. When the oil shimmers, add half of the sausage patties and cook, flipping once, until deeply browned and cooked through, 3 to 4 minutes per side. Transfer to a plate and tent with foil. Wipe the skillet clean, and repeat with the remaining 1 tablespoon olive oil and sausage patties.

Note

Since this yields a large batch of sausage, it makes sense to freeze half in order to have them on hand for another time. Simply form all of the patties, cook however many you need, and wrap the remaining patties (raw) in freezer-safe plastic wrap, then freeze in an airtight container for up to 3 months. Thaw in the refrigerator overnight before cooking.

Farmer's Sausage, Egg & Cheese Sandwiches

Serves 4   I love a good, savory handheld (well, sort of!) breakfast and can't imagine turning down a flavorful sausage, egg, and cheese sandwich for anything else. As a kid I detested cereal and milk, especially all-bran flakes with banana that Mom would sometimes put before me with a hopeful look in her eyes. I ate those dutifully to please her, but what I really wanted was her breakfast sandwich made with leftover boerewors. Layered with egg, tomato, cheese, and apricot chutney, the sandwich had everything going for it: sweet, salty, cheesy, toasty, and so satisfying to bite into. This is my re-creation, made with Farmer's Sausage Patties (page 191) as a shortcut for the boerewors. The flavors are an almost exact replica of Mom's sandwiches, swapping out toasted white bread for brioche and adding some peppery arugula to give this rich breakfast a fresh, peppery kick.

1 tablespoon extra-virgin olive oil

4 uncooked Farmer's Sausage Patties (page 191)

1 tablespoon unsalted butter

4 large eggs

½ cup Sheba (page 188) or chunky mild salsa, divided

4 brioche buns, toasted

2 cups loosely packed arugula

4 slices Gouda cheese

¼ cup District Six Apricot Chutney (page 263), or Mrs. H.S. Ball's Peach Chutney (available online)

1   Preheat the oven to warm.

2   In a large skillet, heat the oil over medium heat. When the oil shimmers, add the sausage patties and cook, undisturbed, until deeply browned and cooked through, 3 to 4 minutes per side. Transfer to a plate and keep warm in the oven.

3   Wipe out the skillet, and reduce the heat to medium-low. Add the butter, and let it melt. Crack in the eggs one at a time, and cook until the whites are just starting to set, about 2 minutes. Remove the skillet from the heat and let sit, covered, until the egg whites are set and the yolks are custardy, about 5 minutes.

4   Spoon 3 tablespoons of the sheba onto the bottom half of each bun, then top each with some arugula, a farmer's sausage patty, a slice of Gouda, and a fried egg. Spread 1 tablespoon of the apricot chutney onto each top bun and close the sandwiches. Serve immediately.

Hot-Smoked Salmon Egg Bites

Serves 4 (12 egg bites) The city of Brookhaven, Mississippi, is small, with a large sign off the interstate exit that reads "Homeseekers Paradise." If you take a stroll down the historic part of town, you'll see beautiful antebellum and Victorian homes with pecan trees lining the sidewalks and friendly neighbors walking their dogs. My husband and I settled here mostly because I fell in love with our gingerbread house—an impulse buy after scrolling through real estate apps late at night. Come to think of it, a house alone should probably not be the deciding factor on where to live, but nevertheless, it worked out for us.

On weekend mornings, we take a leisurely stroll downtown for coffee, and wonder whether opening our own quaint breakfast spot could work. As we walk, we scope out locations and discuss renovations (all while knowing that it'll be the end of our sanity!). These New York bagel–inspired egg bites loaded with hot-smoked salmon and goat cheese—hold the bagels—are a strong contender for the hypothetical menu. As a bonus, they have that easy-but-a-little-bit-fancy vibe I'm (probably never) going for. If I include the recipe here, they'll live on despite our decision (my mind is made up).

Brookhaven is nothing like the iconic cities that intrigue most people about the US, but life is sweet, and dreams are big here in small-town Mississippi.

Olive oil spray

8-ounce fillet hot-smoked salmon, flaked

½ cup (4 ounces) crumbled goat cheese

1 tablespoon chopped fresh chives

10 large eggs

1 cup (8 ounces) cottage cheese

1 teaspoon everything bagel seasoning

FOR SERVING (OPTIONAL)

Crème fraîche

Easy Pickled Red Onions (page 256)

Capers

Fresh dill fronds, for garnish

1 Preheat the oven to 350°F with a rack in the center position.

2 Spray a 12-cup muffin tin with olive oil spray, and set it inside a large rimmed sheet pan deep enough to hold at least 2 cups of water. Divide the smoked salmon, goat cheese, and chives among the muffin cups.

3 In a large bowl, whisk together the eggs, cottage cheese, and everything bagel seasoning until well combined and frothy. Pour into the muffin tin, leaving about ¼ inch of space at the top of each cup. Transfer to the oven, then pour 2 cups of water into the sheet pan. Bake until the egg bites are set and light golden brown on top, 16 to 18 minutes. Carefully remove from the oven and use a fork to gently lift each egg bite out.

4 Serve on plates with a dollop of crème fraîche, pickled red onions, and capers, and garnish with dill fronds, if desired.

Steak & Cheesy Egg Breakfast Tacos

Serves 4   I vaguely recall the South African comedian Trevor Noah once saying that Mexican people never came to South Africa. While the Mexican influence on the States is huge, Mexican and Tex-Mex cuisine had not made its way to the rainbow nation until very recently. I knew nothing of tacos until my late twenties. My first taste of Tex-Mex cooking was a Taco Bell burrito in South Korea on the day the very first branch opened there, way back in 2010. I stood in line for hours along with other expats, who either missed eating this food or were curious about it like I was.

Was I let down by that burrito? Yes, indeed. It wasn't the greatest, but I wanted to know more about Tex-Mex flavors, and it just so happened that I moved to El Paso, Texas, one year later, when my husband got stationed at Fort Bliss. There, fully immersed in the vibrant community on the border, I ate delicious Tex-Mex cuisine to my heart's content. I eventually incorporated some of those flavors into my own cooking. Now, I wake up some mornings thinking about how to make the ultimate breakfast taco. Cheesy scrambled eggs tucked into warm corn tortillas with sliced steak, store-bought pico de gallo, and a creamy avocado jalapeño sauce is my go-to. Just the thought of these motivates me to get the day started.

AVOCADO SAUCE
½ cup sour cream

½ cup roughly chopped fresh cilantro leaves and tender stems

1 large avocado, pitted and sliced

1 small jalapeño, seeded

2 tablespoons fresh lime juice

¼ teaspoon kosher salt

EGGS
8 large eggs

1 teaspoon kosher salt, divided

2 tablespoons unsalted butter

¼ small yellow onion, finely chopped

1 garlic clove, minced

½ teaspoon ground cumin

½ teaspoon freshly ground black pepper

1 cup shredded Cheddar cheese

FOR SERVING
8 corn tortillas, warmed

1 cup pico de gallo

Leftover sliced steak (such as page 146) or cooked chorizo crumbles

½ cup loosely packed fresh cilantro leaves (optional)

Hot sauce (optional)

1   TO MAKE THE AVOCADO SAUCE, in a high-speed blender, blend the sour cream, cilantro, avocado, jalapeño, lime juice, and salt until very smooth; thin with 1 to 2 tablespoons water if needed.

2   TO COOK THE EGGS, in a large bowl, whisk together the eggs and ½ teaspoon of the salt until well combined.

3   In a large skillet, heat the butter over medium heat. Once the butter foams, add the onion, garlic, cumin, pepper, and the remaining ½ teaspoon salt; cook, stirring occasionally, until the onion is translucent and the cumin is fragrant, 1 to 2 minutes.

4   Reduce the heat to medium-low. Pour the eggs over the onion and cook, stirring occasionally with a rubber spatula to incorporate the eggs and onion evenly, until the eggs are just set, 2 to 3 minutes. Stir in the cheese.

5   Spoon some of the avocado jalapeño sauce onto each tortilla, then add some cooked eggs on top of each one, dividing evenly. Serve with the pico de gallo, and sliced steak or chorizo. Sprinkle with the cilantro before serving, and pass the hot sauce at the table, if desired.

All About the Feta Frittata

Serves 4   Greek salad is the single most popular salad in South Africa because it's easy, delicious, and features ingredients widely cultivated in our Mediterranean climate. My all-time favorite place to visit for a good Greek salad is Ocean Basket, a popular seafood restaurant in Cape Town. There, they serve artfully arranged platters of grilled shrimp, fresh fish, tender calamari, and buttery mussels on heaps of savory yellow rice with the house Greek salad on the side. The salad has always been the highlight of the meal for me because of the generous amount of Kalamata olives and the gargantuan chunk of nutty sheep's milk feta plopped on top. It's something that I could eat for breakfast, lunch, and dinner. This anytime frittata with those Mediterranean flavors gives me the green light to do that.

8 large eggs

⅓ cup dry-packed sun-dried tomatoes, roughly chopped

¼ cup cottage cheese

¼ cup sliced Kalamata olives

1 teaspoon dried oregano

¼ teaspoon red pepper flakes

6 ounces sheep's milk feta cheese, cubed, divided

2 tablespoons extra-virgin olive oil

1 small red onion, halved and thinly sliced

2 large garlic cloves

2 cups tightly packed baby spinach

3 tablespoons red wine vinegar, divided

1 cup cherry tomatoes, quartered

1 Persian cucumber, diced

Kosher salt and freshly cracked black pepper

¼ cup loosely packed chopped fresh herbs, such as dill, chives, parsley, or oregano leaves

1   Preheat the oven to 350°F with a rack in the center position.

2   In a large bowl, whisk together the eggs, sun-dried tomatoes, cottage cheese, olives, dried oregano, red pepper flakes, and half of the feta. Set aside.

3   In an 8- to 10-inch ovenproof skillet, heat the oil over medium heat. When the oil shimmers, add the onion and garlic, and cook, stirring occasionally until the onion is translucent and the garlic is fragrant, 2 to 3 minutes. Add the spinach and 2 tablespoons of the red wine vinegar, and cook, stirring often, until the spinach is wilted and the liquid has completely evaporated, 1 to 2 minutes. Reduce the heat to medium-low.

4   Pour the egg mixture into the skillet, and stir gently with a rubber spatula to evenly distribute the onion and spinach. Cook until the edges just start to set, 3 to 4 minutes. Arrange the remaining feta cheese on top. Transfer the skillet to the oven, and bake until the frittata is almost set on top, 10 to 12 minutes. Remove from the oven, cover, and let sit for 5 minutes to finish cooking.

5   Slide the frittata onto a cutting board and slice into wedges. In a small bowl, toss the tomatoes and cucumber with the remaining 1 tablespoon vinegar; season with salt and black pepper. Spoon over the frittata and top with the herbs.

Corn Fritters with Fried Eggs & Hot Honey

Serves 4   This is my Southern take on the corn fritters that I grew up eating for breakfast at Grandma's house. Instead of keeping it simple as she did, I take a maximalist approach and add a (sneaky) selection of chopped vegetables, plus enough cheese and crisp-cooked bacon to make the fritters extra delicious. The addition of fried eggs, peppery watercress, creamy avocado, and sweet vine-ripened tomatoes round out the meal and perhaps tip the scale back toward that sweet spot between naughty and nice. Hit the corn fritters with a drizzle of hot honey, and you've got a well-balanced breakfast, brunch, lunch, or breakfast-for-dinner.

CORN FRITTERS
½ cup self-rising flour

¼ cup buttermilk

1 large egg

1 tablespoon unsalted butter, softened

1 teaspoon Cajun seasoning

1 (15.25-ounce) can whole-kernel corn, drained

1 cup shredded zucchini (about 1 small zucchini)

½ cup shredded Pepper Jack cheese

½ cup finely chopped collard greens or kale (stems and tough ribs removed)

¼ cup finely chopped roasted red bell pepper

4 slices crisp-cooked bacon, chopped

2 green onions, finely chopped

2 large garlic cloves, minced

4 tablespoons extra-virgin olive oil, divided

EGGS
1 tablespoon unsalted butter

4 large eggs

Kosher salt and freshly ground black pepper

FOR SERVING
Cherry tomatoes on the vine (optional)

1 large avocado, pitted and cut into wedges (optional)

1 cup loosely packed watercress, arugula, or other tender greens, such as baby spinach (optional)

Hot honey (see Notes) or hot sauce

1   TO MAKE THE FRITTERS, in a large bowl, combine the flour, buttermilk, egg, butter, and Cajun seasoning, and stir with a fork until you have a thick batter. Add the corn, zucchini, cheese, collard greens, bell pepper, bacon, green onions, and garlic, and stir until evenly distributed throughout the batter.

2   In a large nonstick skillet, heat 2 tablespoons of the olive oil over medium-high heat. Working with half the batter, fry ¼ cupfuls until the fritters are lightly golden brown and crisp, about 2 minutes per side. Transfer to a paper towel–lined plate and tent with aluminum foil to keep warm. Continue frying the remaining batter in the remaining 2 tablespoons olive oil.

3   TO COOK THE EGGS, in the same skillet, melt the butter over medium heat. When the butter starts to sizzle, gently crack in the eggs and fry for 2 minutes, then remove from the heat and let sit, covered, until the whites are set and the yolks are custardy, 3 to 5 minutes. Season with salt and pepper.

4   TO SERVE, divide the corn fritters among plates and serve with the fried eggs, cherry tomatoes, avocado wedges, and watercress, if using. Pass some hot honey or hot sauce at the table.

Note
You can buy hot honey or make your own by mixing ¼ cup of honey with 1 tablespoon of Tabasco.

Fun Twist
The corn fritters are also delicious on their own with sour cream, lime wedges, thinly sliced jalapeño, and cilantro.

Spiced Brown Sugar Bacon

Serves 4   Once you start adding a little sweetness and spice to bacon, it's hard to go back. With just a few ingredients, the salty, smoky strips are transformed into a treat that you can enjoy as a snack, for breakfast, or chopped to sprinkle over salads. This is much easier than glazing bacon and having to flip halfway through cooking, with the only trade-off being that the brown sugar won't fully melt. I'm totally fine with that!

3 tablespoons packed light brown sugar

¼ teaspoon cayenne pepper

½ pound thick-cut sliced bacon

1 tablespoon Dijon mustard

1   Preheat the oven to 375°F with a rack in the center position. Line a rimmed sheet pan with parchment paper.

2   In a small bowl, stir together the brown sugar and cayenne pepper.

3   Arrange the bacon on the prepared sheet pan in a single layer, and brush half of the Dijon mustard evenly onto one side, then sprinkle with half of the spiced brown sugar. Flip the bacon, and repeat with the remaining Dijon mustard and brown sugar. Bake until lightly browned and crisp in spots, watching carefully so that the bacon does not burn, 18 to 20 minutes. Transfer the bacon to a paper towel–lined plate, and serve immediately.

SPICED BROWN SUGAR BACON, 199

seven

VEGETABLE HEAVY

Forgotten Greens Mac & Cheese

Serves 8 DJ's grandpa was old-school cool, and I knew I liked his style the minute we first met at Thanksgiving dinner: confident, set in his ways, but loving and warm. During our initial introduction, I couldn't pick up his heavy southern Louisiana dialect, and thus was unable to converse with him to the point of frustration. He just smiled, and I buried my head in DJ's shoulder, very embarrassed. As we later gathered around the most magnificent spread of slow-cooked pot roast, greens, sweetened yams, and mac and cheese, suddenly everyone spoke the same language. I like to think of this mac and cheese as the heart of the meal when I do serve it, in remembrance of Grandpa. It's soul food, it's home food, it's family food. Inspired by two of the sides from Grandpa's dinner, this recipe also has a nifty trick for using any leafy green vegetables forgotten in the crisper drawer. Finely chop them and toast with some panko to add a little extra crunch to the baked macaroni once it comes out of the oven. The panko is also excellent as a topper for other pasta dishes, or roasted vegetables!

Kosher salt

1 pound macaroni or cavatappi

1 tablespoon extra-virgin olive oil

1 cup finely chopped greens, such as kale, mustard greens, collards, Brussels sprouts, or Swiss chard

1 cup panko bread crumbs

½ teaspoon garlic powder

1 stick (8 tablespoons) salted butter

½ cup all-purpose flour

4 cups whole milk

¼ teaspoon cayenne pepper

¼ teaspoon freshly grated nutmeg (or substitute ground nutmeg)

4 ounces Velveeta cheese, cubed

4 ounces freshly grated Parmesan cheese

1 pound sharp Cheddar cheese, freshly shredded, divided (see Note)

Kosher salt and freshly ground black pepper

1 Bring a large pot of salted water to a rolling boil over medium-high heat. Add the pasta, give it a good stir, and cook according to the package directions until 2 minutes shy of al dente. Drain, and set aside.

2 While the pasta cooks, in a large nonstick skillet, heat the olive oil over medium heat. Once the oil shimmers, add the greens, panko, and garlic powder, and cook, stirring often, until the panko is toasted and some of the greens are crispy, 2 to 3 minutes. Remove from the heat, and let cool.

3 Preheat the oven to broil with a rack in the center position.

4 In a large saucepan, melt the butter over medium heat. When the butter just starts to brown, add the flour and cook, stirring often, until all the butter is absorbed and the flour smells nutty, 1 to 2 minutes. Whisking constantly, slowly pour in 2 cups of the milk in a thin, steady stream and cook until combined and smooth. Add the remaining 3 cups milk and cook, stirring often, until smooth and thick enough to coat the back of a spoon, 5 to 6 minutes. Stir in the cayenne and nutmeg.

5 Remove the saucepan from the heat, then add the Velveeta, Parmesan, and three-fourths of the Cheddar and stir until completely incorporated into the sauce. Add the cooked pasta and stir until well coated, then season with salt and black pepper.

6 Transfer the pasta to a 3- to 4-quart baking dish and smooth the top into an even layer. Sprinkle with the remaining Cheddar, and broil until golden and bubbly, 4 to 5 minutes. Let cool for 5 minutes, then serve with the toasted greens panko.

Note

It's better to buy your cheese in blocks and shred it yourself because the preshredded stuff is usually coated in starch to prevent clumping. That same starch might also prevent your cheese from reaching its full melting potential, so shred your own!

Pimento Cheese Tomato Pie Galette

Serves 2 to 4   When my husband, DJ, and I first purchased our home, it was a proud moment for us—a couple of twentysomethings who had worked so hard to make possible the day that a Realtor would put some keys in our hands. It was a pink gingerbread house built in 1897, previously owned by an artist, Miss Dixie. She had lovingly created the home of her dreams by painting murals on every wall in the house over the course of twenty years: a gray cat next to the front door, rural scenes with red-roofed barns on hidden pocket doors, the African Serengeti in the hallway (a sign!), and tiny ceramic mice gently glued into the holes of the reclaimed bathroom doors. When we toured the place for the first time, my soul felt at ease, and Miss Dixie and I cried in the kitchen as I promised to love it just as she did. In our excitement, DJ and I immediately put an offer on the house and were lucky enough to move in not long after. Sometime later, a greeting card arrived in the mail with the words "Enjoy your new, old house! ~ Miss Dixie." And we have.

In the beginning, getting to discover the little nooks and crannies that I failed to notice in our haste felt like a wonderful treasure hunt to me. While cleaning the tallest shelf in the hallway, I found a note that Miss Dixie's husband had written to her, hoping that she would find it while painting, perhaps. "I love you, have a great day! ~ David." Two tickets to a college basketball game in 2011 that must've held a lot of meaning to them, Mod Podged onto a sideboard in the hallway. In the kitchen cabinets, a collection of decoupaged recipes like "Copper Pennies," "Green Bean Casserole," and also a very quintessentially Southern recipe for tomato pie.

That pie was the inspiration for this delicious galette. Most tomato pies layer fresh tomatoes with a blend of shredded cheese and mayonnaise, but I take a little shortcut by using another Southern staple, pimento cheese. When summer rolls around and the worst of the heat moves from the front of the house, we sit on the porch next to the painted cat, with slices of this rustic pie, and feel very thankful to own such a lovely, old home.

CRUST

1¼ cups all-purpose flour, plus more for dusting

1 stick (8 tablespoons) cold salted butter, cubed

1 teaspoon Italian seasoning

2 tablespoons ice water, plus more if needed

1 tablespoon white wine vinegar

1 large egg, lightly beaten

2 tablespoons freshly grated Parmesan cheese (optional)

FILLING

2 large ripe but firm heirloom or beefsteak tomatoes (about 1 pound), cut into ½-inch-thick slices

½ teaspoon kosher salt

1 cup Peppadew & Gouda Pimento Cheese (page 48), or store-bought (I like Palmetto brand)

1 large shallot, thinly sliced

1 cup halved (quartered, if large) cherry tomatoes

¼ cup torn fresh basil leaves (optional)

Flaky salt and freshly ground black pepper

1   TO MAKE THE CRUST, in a food processor, combine the flour, butter, and Italian seasoning and pulse until coarse, sandy crumbs form, about 15 seconds. Add the ice water and vinegar, pulsing until the dough just comes together, about 30 seconds. To test whether the dough is ready, pinch some dough between your fingers. If the dough holds together, it's ready. If it's still crumbly, add the extra ice water 1 teaspoon at a time, pulsing in between, until the dough comes together. Transfer the dough to a lightly floured work surface, and gently form into a 4-inch disc. Wrap in plastic wrap and refrigerate for at least 1 hour, up to 2 days.

2   TO PREPARE THE FILLING, on a paper towel–lined sheet pan, arrange the sliced tomatoes in a single layer and sprinkle with the kosher salt. Cover with another layer of paper towels and let sit for 30 minutes. Pat the excess moisture dry with paper towels.

3   Preheat the oven to 400°F with a rack in the center position.

4   Place the dough between two sheets of parchment paper, and roll into a 12-inch round. Peel off the top parchment, and transfer the parchment with the pastry to a large sheet pan. Leaving a 1½-inch border around the edges, spread the pimento cheese onto the round of dough. Arrange the sliced tomatoes and shallot on top (some overlap is okay). Fold the border over the filling, pleating where needed and leaving the center of the galette exposed. Brush the pastry with the beaten egg and sprinkle with the Parmesan, if using.

5   Bake until the pastry is golden brown and the filling is bubbling, 35 to 40 minutes. Let cool for 10 minutes, then scatter the cherry tomatoes and basil, if using, over the filling. Season with flaky salt and pepper.

Tteok alla Vodka

Serves 4   DJ will trade any noodle or pasta shape for *tteok*, the cylindrical rice cakes that we ate during late-night dates at stalls along the Han River in South Korea. There, the chewy rice cakes are simmered in a vibrantly red sweet and spicy gochujang-based sauce in a dish called *tteokbokki*, a very popular street food. This recipe takes inspiration from tteokbokki and uses tteok in place of penne for a toothsome Korean-Italian riff on penne alla vodka.

1 pound (2-inch-long) cylindrical tteok (rice cakes; see Note)

2 tablespoons extra-virgin olive oil

1 small onion, chopped

4 large garlic cloves, minced

½ cup vodka

2 cups marinara sauce (I like Rao's)

½ cup Chicken Stock (page 259) or low-sodium chicken broth, or vegetable broth to make vegetarian

¼ cup heavy cream

¼ cup freshly grated Parmesan cheese

1 teaspoon kosher salt

½ teaspoon red pepper flakes, plus more if needed

Torn fresh Italian herbs, such as oregano, parsley, and basil leaves, for serving

1   Bring a large pot of salted water to a boil over medium-high heat. Once the water gallops, add the tteok and cook, stirring occasionally, until softened, 2 to 3 minutes, 1 to 2 minutes longer if using frozen tteok. Drain, and set aside.

2   In a large Dutch oven, heat the oil over medium heat. Once the oil shimmers, add the onion and cook, stirring occasionally, until translucent, 3 to 4 minutes. Add the garlic and stir until fragrant, about 30 seconds more. Add the vodka and cook until the liquid is reduced by half, 1 to 2 minutes. Add the marinara sauce, chicken stock, and cream, then stir in the tteok. Remove from the heat and stir in the Parmesan, letting the residual heat melt the cheese.

3   Serve the tteok with torn fresh herbs scattered on top.

Note

You can find tteok in the refrigerated or frozen section of most Asian grocery stores. If you've never had it before, expect them to be much chewier than noodles. Fresh tteok only takes a few minutes in boiling water to soften, and will float once ready to drain. To test for doneness, pierce one with a fork. You should be able to do so easily. They will continue to soak up the sauce as they sit and will harden as the sauce cools, so this dish is best eaten soon after it's made. To reheat, simply add ½ cup of water, then simmer and stir over medium heat until the tteok softens again.

Sun-Dried Tomato & Olive Buttermilk Quick Bread

Makes 1 (9 x 5-inch) loaf (about 8 servings)

My mom would make a bread using a packet of white onion soup mix, to serve with my dad's vegetable-heavy soups. This adaptation, inspired by hers, relies on some pantry staples instead of that powdered soup mix. While I like to bake, I start to get nervous around recipes that mention yeast, so those who share a similar aversion can rest assured, this quick bread is a breeze to make with zero yeast in sight. The sun-dried tomatoes and Castelvetrano olives provide little pockets of tang and mild brininess to every slice, with Parmesan cheese deepening the flavor that originally came from the soup packet.

This bread is highly customizable, too: You can swap out the olives or tomatoes with chopped, cooked vegetables and finely chopped fresh greens, and replace the herbs with any kind that you prefer.

Unsalted butter, for greasing, plus grass-fed butter, for serving (optional)

2¼ cups all-purpose flour

2 teaspoons baking powder

1 teaspoon dried parsley

1 teaspoon dried thyme

1 teaspoon kosher salt

1 teaspoon freshly ground black pepper

½ teaspoon baking soda

½ teaspoon dry mustard (I like Colman's English mustard)

¾ cup freshly grated Parmesan cheese

½ cup pitted Castelvetrano olives, chopped

¼ cup dry-packed sun-dried tomatoes, finely chopped

1 green onion, minced

2 extra-large eggs

1¼ cups buttermilk

1½ tablespoons extra-virgin olive oil

1 Preheat the oven to 350°F. Grease a 9 × 5-inch loaf tin with butter or line with parchment paper.

2 In a large bowl, whisk together the flour, baking powder, parsley, thyme, salt, pepper, baking soda, and dry mustard until thoroughly combined. Stir in the Parmesan, olives, sun-dried tomatoes, and green onion.

3 In a separate large bowl, whisk the eggs, then whisk in the buttermilk and oil until frothy, about 1 minute.

4 Use a wooden spoon to make a well in the center of the flour mixture and stir in the wet ingredients until just combined. Scrape the batter into the prepared loaf tin.

5 Bake until the top of the loaf is light golden brown and a fine skewer inserted into the middle of the loaf comes out clean, 40 to 45 minutes. Tip the bread out onto a wire rack. This is hard, but let the bread cool slightly before slicing and spreading with butter, if desired. Serve with your favorite soups or toasted as a snack. Store any remaining bread in an airtight container at room temperature for up to 3 days, or sliced and separated with sheets of parchment paper in an airtight container in the freezer for up to 2 months.

Risotto with Roasted Cauliflower & Lemon

Serves 4 as a main, 6 as a side Inspired by my mom's cauliflower gratin, this risotto allows me to enjoy cauliflower and cheese as a standalone dinner (it's also great as a hearty side dish). Aged goat Gouda adds depth of flavor to the creamy rice, with the lemony cauliflower and crunchy toasted nuts providing acidity and textural contrast to balance out the meal.

ROASTED CAULIFLOWER

1 pound cauliflower florets, cut into bite-size pieces (no larger than 1 inch), if necessary

1 small lemon, halved lengthwise and thinly sliced crosswise

¼ cup extra-virgin olive oil

1 tablespoon white balsamic vinegar

1 tablespoon whole fresh rosemary needles

1 teaspoon kosher salt

½ teaspoon freshly ground black pepper

RISOTTO

4 cups Chicken Stock (page 259), low-sodium chicken broth, or vegetable broth if making it vegetarian

1 cup water

2 tablespoons extra-virgin olive oil

1 small yellow onion, minced

2 garlic cloves, minced

1 cup arborio rice

½ cup dry white wine, such as Sauvignon Blanc

2 tablespoons salted butter, softened

2 ounces aged goat Gouda or Parmesan cheese, freshly grated

¼ cup toasted pine nuts and/or hazelnuts, for serving (see Note)

1 TO MAKE THE ROASTED CAULIFLOWER, preheat the oven to 425°F with a rack in the center position.

2 On a rimmed sheet pan, toss the cauliflower with the lemon, olive oil, balsamic vinegar, rosemary, salt, and pepper until evenly coated. Roast until tender, stirring halfway through, about 25 minutes.

3 MEANWHILE, TO MAKE THE RISOTTO, in a medium saucepan, combine the chicken stock and water and bring to a gentle simmer over low heat.

4 In a large saucepan, heat the oil over medium heat. Add the onion and garlic, and cook, stirring occasionally, until the onion just starts to soften and the garlic is fragrant, 2 to 3 minutes. Add the rice and stir until the grains are translucent at the edges and start to smell toasted, about 2 minutes. Add the wine and cook, stirring often, until evaporated, about 1 minute.

5 Add the hot stock 1 ladleful (about ½ cup) at a time and cook, stirring often, until completely absorbed after each addition and the rice is creamy, 18 to 20 minutes. Reduce the heat to low, then stir in the butter and cheese until melted.

6 Ladle the risotto into bowls, then top with the roasted cauliflower and lemon slices. Sprinkle with the toasted pine nuts and serve.

Note

To toast nuts on the stovetop, heat a large skillet over medium-high. Once hot, add the nuts in a single layer and cook, stirring occasionally, until fragrant and golden, 3 to 5 minutes for pine nuts or 5 to 7 minutes for hazelnuts. Toasted nuts are also available for sale at stores like Trader Joe's.

Okonomiyaki Cabbage "Steaks"

Serves 4   This vegetable-forward main course takes inspiration from *okonomiyaki*, a savory Japanese pancake with shredded cabbage, meat, seafood or other ingredients in the batter. In this pancake-less riff, I drape bacon on thick slabs of green cabbage, then roast them until the bacon is crisp and the frilly outer leaves are slightly charred. The unexpected "steaks" are a fun way to showcase cabbage, and become even more delicious with traditional okonomiyaki toppings: furikake, bonito flakes, fruity barbecue sauce, and Kewpie mayonnaise.

When I was undergoing IVF treatments and couldn't have flour, I turned to this version when the okonomiyaki cravings hit. The original dish is fantastic, and I encourage anyone who hasn't tried it to seek it out. I do think, however, this adapted way of cooking captures the essence of the Japanese word *okonomiyaki*, which in English translates to "grilled as you like it" or "things you like, grilled." Anything goes! To make a vegetarian version of these steaks, see the notes at the end of the recipe for guidance.

CABBAGE STEAKS
4 (¾-inch-thick) slabs of cabbage, cut from the center

4 slices thick-cut uncured bacon, halved crosswise (see Notes)

OKONOMIYAKI SAUCE (SEE NOTES)
½ cup no-sugar-added ketchup

⅓ cup Worcestershire sauce

¼ cup oyster sauce

3 tablespoons pure maple syrup, plus more to taste

½ teaspoon shichimi togarashi (Japanese chili and spice blend available at Asian markets and online) or red pepper flakes (optional)

FOR SERVING (SEE NOTES)
Kewpie mayonnaise

Kimchi furikake or nori komi furikake

Bonito flakes

Green onions, thinly sliced at an angle

1   Preheat the oven to 425°F with a rack in the center position.

2   **TO MAKE THE CABBAGE STEAKS**, line a large rimmed sheet pan with parchment paper, place the cabbage on top, then top each slab with 2 pieces of the bacon. If your cabbage is dense, add ¼ cup of water to the sheet pan. Cover with foil and roast, basting the cabbage with the melted bacon fat halfway through, until the bacon is crisp, the edges of the cabbage are deep golden brown, and the centers are crisp-tender when pierced with a fork, about 20 minutes. If needed, remove the foil and roast until the bacon is crisp, 5 minutes more.

3   **MEANWHILE, TO MAKE THE OKONOMIYAKI SAUCE**, in a small bowl, stir together the ketchup, Worcestershire sauce, oyster sauce, maple syrup, and *shichimi togarashi*, if using, until well combined.

4   **TO SERVE**, Transfer the cabbage steaks to plates, and drizzle about 3 tablespoons of the okonomiyaki sauce evenly over each one. Squeeze thin stripes of Kewpie mayo on top in a zigzag pattern, and sprinkle with a light dusting of furikake, bonito flakes, and green onions. Serve immediately.

Notes
If you prefer to make these cabbage steaks vegan or vegetarian, leave out the bacon and roast the cabbage steaks after drizzling with ¼ cup of extra-virgin olive oil. Use your favorite vegan mayonnaise, oyster sauce, Worcestershire sauce, and furikake, and omit the bonito flakes.

Kewpie mayonnaise is a little sweeter than American mayo, but another kind is okay if you don't have it!

Furikake is also sometimes referred to as Japanese rice seasoning, and if unavailable, it can be replaced with roasted seaweed snacks—just crush them by hand before sprinkling.

Bonito flakes are thinly shaved dried smoked fish that can be found in the Asian section of most good grocery stores. You can leave it out—just add more furikake or roasted seaweed.

Wild Rice Bowls with Roasted Beets, Goat Cheese & Preserved Lemon Drizzle

Serves 4   Beets are polarizing to many—you either hate them or love them—and if you're in camp "beets taste like dirt," then the discovery of milder, sweeter (stainproof!) golden beets might just change your mind. I roast them in a Dutch oven instead of using foil, with fresh bay leaves, rosemary, and thick slices of sweet onion that caramelize the bottom of the pot. Wild rice, peppery salad greens, and big chunks of goat cheese play more than supporting roles; each element is delicious in its own right. The hearty vegetarian rice bowls are drizzled with a lively preserved lemon vinaigrette right before serving, and the brightness just makes everything pop.

BEETS

1 large yellow onion, cut into ½-inch-thick slices

6 to 8 medium golden beets, trimmed and scrubbed (about 2 pounds)

¼ cup water

2 tablespoons extra-virgin olive oil

1 teaspoon coarse sea salt or kosher salt

2 fresh rosemary sprigs

2 fresh bay leaves

WILD RICE

1 cup wild rice, rinsed

3 cups water

½ teaspoon kosher salt

1 tablespoon extra-virgin olive oil

VINAIGRETTE

3 tablespoons extra-virgin olive oil

2 tablespoons fresh lemon juice

1 tablespoon pure maple syrup

1 tablespoon Dijon mustard

1 tablespoon chopped rind from preserved lemons, homemade (page 258) or store-bought

¼ teaspoon freshly ground black pepper

FOR SERVING

4 cups mixed peppery greens, such as watercress, radicchio, and arugula

8 ounces fresh goat cheese, broken into large chunks

1   ROAST THE BEETS: Preheat the oven to 400°F with a rack in the center position.

2   Line the bottom of a large Dutch oven with the onion slices, then arrange the beets on top. Add the water, olive oil, coarse salt, rosemary, and bay leaves. Roast, covered, until the beets are fork-tender and the onion is slightly caramelized, 45 to 50 minutes.

3   MEANWHILE, COOK THE RICE: In a medium saucepan, combine the rice, water, salt, and olive oil, and bring to a boil over medium-high heat. Reduce the heat to low and cook, covered, stirring occasionally, until the grains are tender and the water is absorbed, 40 to 45 minutes. You'll know the rice is ready when some of the grains start to break.

4   MAKE THE VINAIGRETTE: In a pint jar, combine the olive oil, lemon juice, maple syrup, mustard, preserved lemon rind, and pepper. Cover and shake vigorously until emulsified.

5   Once the beets are just cool enough to handle, peel the skin and trim away any tough parts near the stems. Scoop out the caramelized onion and stir into the rice, if desired. Discard the rosemary sprigs and bay leaves. Cut the beets into bite-size pieces.

6   FOR SERVING: Divide the rice, greens, beets, and goat cheese among bowls. Drizzle each with a few tablespoons of the preserved lemon vinaigrette, and serve.

Golden Tomato Soup

Serves 2   In a very distinct memory of my mother in the nineties, we are months into living in Vanderbijlpark, a predominantly white middle-class suburb west of Johannesburg, after moving there for my dad's job. It was post-apartheid, but the effects of segregation still loomed in the air. None of the neighbors have said hello. Mom is sitting at a table outside in the sun wearing a yellow sundress and eating fruit, foraged from the sprawling garden, sprinkled with salt. Yellow tomatoes, loquats, gooseberries, lemons, or quince—the fruit I vaguely recall doesn't even matter. In that moment she is her truest self, her shiny new bob haircut flipping around as she flicks her bangs away to glance over at my sisters and me. We are playing with the hose, wearing blue pinstripe shorts and yellow T-shirts to match Mom's dress, watching carefully as the water forges through the grass, forcing bugs to crawl up from the bottom. Beetles, grasshoppers, chafers, and skippers—they were our little pets and kept us occupied. "Don't harm them, be gentle," she would say. "Here comes the ice cream van! Buy us some Jolly Jellies!"

Mom clearly was a free spirit who made our home a place of exploration and fun no matter what went on outside those gates or in her mind. She had studied art and education in college but never made a career out of teaching. When I was in high school, she was a cash office clerk at the local grocery store. When she met my dad she worked as a salesperson at OK Bazaar, a furniture store. Before that, from the time she was eight, she baked cookies to sell for extra money. In Johannesburg, her job was taking care of us while Dad worked at night and slept during the day. I wonder what it must've been like to have three girls and to be that alone, far away from the familiarity of Cape Town where she grew up, where people looked like us and we weren't treated differently. Even when things got tough and prepackaged soup was all Mom could manage to put on the table, she made

life fun, she cheered us on, and allowed us the freedom to express ourselves. "Why not play with your food?" would start turning the wheels in our minds during mealtime. "As long as you also eat it" would prompt us to stop and think about our choices in a nice way. She was, and still is, that kind of mom.

While you could absolutely make this soup with red tomatoes, I jump at the chance to make it with yellow tomatoes in late summer. The golden hue reminds me of my strong and resilient mother and the classic bowls of comfort that cheered us up and kept us going back then. It's a taste from a moment of childhood innocence when the world was all right and the only thing that mattered was that we were loved.

2 pounds yellow tomatoes (about 6 large), quartered

1 medium yellow bell pepper, quartered

4 shallots, peeled and halved

8 large garlic cloves, peeled and left whole

2 teaspoons dried oregano or marjoram

2 teaspoons dried basil

2 teaspoons kosher salt

2 tablespoons extra-virgin olive oil

3 cups vegetable stock

1 tablespoon white balsamic vinegar

1 tablespoon sugar, plus more to taste

¾ cup heavy cream (or 1 cup silken tofu, for a vegan option)

¼ cup crème fraîche (for serving; optional)

Chopped fresh herbs, such as basil, oregano, or thyme leaves, or chives, for serving

continues on page 218

1   Heat the oven to 425°F with a rack in the center position.

2   On a rimmed sheet pan, arrange the tomatoes, bell pepper, shallots, and garlic in an even layer and sprinkle over the dried oregano, dried basil, and salt. Drizzle with the oil and toss to coat. Roast until the shallots are very soft and the tomatoes are slightly caramelized around the edges, 25 to 30 minutes.

3   Transfer the roasted vegetables and any roasting juices on the sheet pan to a large Dutch oven. Add the stock and bring to a boil over medium-high heat. Add the vinegar, sugar, and cream, and stir until the soup is uniformly yellow in color. For a vegan option, replace the cream with the tofu and blend with an immersion blender until very smooth, 1 to 2 minutes.

4   Divide the soup between bowls, top each with half of the crème fraîche, if using, and scatter over the fresh herbs before serving.

Tomato & Onion Grilled Cheese Sandwiches (Braaibroodjies)

Serves 4 Sometimes, to break away from the humdrum of everyday life and get outside in the fall, I take the time to make *braaibroodjies*, South African tomato and onion grilled cheese sandwiches, over the dying embers of a wood fire.

There's a unique sense of connection to the fire for South Africans, it's a part of our fabric and so much more than just a way to cook whatever is on the menu. For hours we stand around the braai, socializing and appreciating every step of the process, from kindling the flame to watching in amazement as the bright orange peaks reach toward the sky. Learning how to make a good fire and tend to food cooked over the flames is a life skill, a rite of passage, and if this task is given to you then you are trusted by those around you.

This tomato and onion grilled cheese is fairly easy to make, but unless you're South African, you might not have had yours like this before. What sets them apart is the added sweetness from chutney, and smoke from the grill—the seventh ingredient in the recipe if you ask me! Since the sandwiches are quite simple, I use the best cheese, butter, and bread I can find.

You could serve braaibroodjies as a side with crispy grilled lamb chops (see page 176), or just as a snack any time, year-round. While I highly recommend cooking them over some coals or a grill for that signature smoked flavor, it's not an expectation, and a skillet is completely okay. Cook as you're able, but please don't forget the chutney! This isn't one of those recipes where everything is measured precisely. It's about the joy of eating a toasty melted cheese sandwich. Sometimes, I add grilled mushrooms, sautéed spinach, and halved Kalamata olives as well. Customize it to your liking and have fun!

8 thick slices sourdough bread

4 tablespoons garlic butter or unsalted butter, softened

¼ cup District Six Apricot Chutney (page 263), Mrs. H.S. Ball's Peach Chutney (available online), or any fruity chutney

8 ounces shredded Gouda cheese

2 large beefsteak or heirloom tomatoes, sliced ¼ inch thick

½ medium red onion, thinly sliced

¼ teaspoon kosher salt

¼ teaspoon freshly ground black pepper

1 Prepare a grill for medium-low heat.

2 Spread each slice of bread with the butter. Place 4 of the slices, buttered-side down, on a work surface or directly onto a grill basket. Top with a layer of chutney, then half of the cheese, then all of the tomatoes and onion. Sprinkle with the salt and pepper, then top with the remaining cheese. Cover with the remaining bread, buttered-side up, and close the grill basket.

3 Grill, flipping occasionally, until the bread is slightly charred around the edges and the cheese is melted, 1½ to 2 minutes per side. Cut each sandwich in half.

Heads-up

If you're cooking over a fire, you'll need a closing wire grill basket to prepare these sandwiches. I've found them online listed as grilled cheese baskets or vegetable baskets. Just make sure that they close tightly enough to hold the sandwiches firmly in place when flipping.

Butternut Squash with Millet, Kale, Dried Fruit & Bacon

Serves 4   I kid you not, someone once composed a playlist of classical music to accompany this hearty main course, because it was, in their own words, "A symphony of flavors that just worked." The reader had served it to her vegetarian(ish) mother for dinner, and they mutually agreed that the bacon was a necessary addition. She wrote a lovely story about it, and I was really happy to know that this cool-weather dish inspired by the foods of my childhood had made such a good impression. The dried fruits evoke the ones I grew up eating after the harvest was over; the squash is a nod to the sun-ripened green pumpkins on the rooftops in my old neighborhood.

The millet can be cooked and stored in the refrigerator for up to 3 days prior to save time. The dried peaches and apricots can be replaced with chopped dates and dried cherries or cranberries based on what you have available. If you prefer to leave the bacon out, I recommend using 2 tablespoons of extra-virgin olive oil to start cooking the onions, then swapping in chopped smoked almonds for the hazelnuts. Though I find a squeeze of fresh lemon juice at serving to add just the right amount of acidity, you could also try it with a lovely Dijon vinaigrette. It's all good.

1 (2-pound) butternut, kabocha squash, or small pumpkin, peeled, seeded, and cut into 1-inch cubes

2 tablespoons extra-virgin olive oil

Kosher salt and freshly ground black pepper

¾ cup raw millet, rinsed and drained (see Note)

1½ cups water or low-sodium vegetable broth

4 slices center-cut bacon, sliced crosswise into ½-inch pieces

½ cup diced red onion

1 tablespoon minced garlic

6 cups chopped kale or Swiss chard (stems and tough ribs removed)

¼ cup finely chopped dried apricots

¼ cup finely chopped dried peaches

½ cup roughly chopped toasted hazelnuts

2 tablespoons fresh lemon juice

1   Preheat the oven to 400°F with a rack in the center position.

2   Place the squash on a large rimmed sheet pan, then drizzle with the olive oil and sprinkle with ¾ teaspoon salt. Toss to coat, and roast until the squash is very tender and the edges are slightly charred, 25 to 30 minutes.

3   Meanwhile, in a medium saucepan over high heat, combine the millet and water. Bring to a rolling boil and cook, stirring occasionally, for 2 minutes. Cook, covered, over low heat, stirring once or twice, until the millet has absorbed all of the water, about 15 minutes. Fluff the millet with a fork and set aside.

4   Heat a large skillet over medium-high heat. Add the bacon and cook, stirring occasionally, until crisp, about 5 minutes. Reduce the heat to medium, add the red onion and garlic, and cook, stirring occasionally, until the onion is soft, 5 to 8 minutes. Add the kale, apricots, and peaches, and cook, stirring often, until the kale is wilted, about 3 minutes. If the skillet looks too dry, add 1 tablespoon of water to help the greens along (the water will evaporate anyway). Season with salt and pepper, then stir in the cooked millet until fully combined.

5   Transfer the millet to a serving platter or dinner plates, and top with the roasted squash and hazelnuts. Drizzle with the lemon juice and serve.

Note

Millet is a gluten-free ancient grain originally from Africa and Asia. It is versatile, nutty in flavor, and cooks quickly. Use it as a substitute for couscous or any other grain, but make sure to rinse it very well before cooking to remove the saponin, the natural bitter coating that acts to protect it from insects and wildlife. To rinse millet, put it in a bowl with water, and move the grains around by hand, scrunching fistfuls at a time until the water is milky. Drain, and repeat the process once more.

Cloudy Day Lentil Soup

Serves 8   The earthy aroma of lentils simmering away on a cloudy day has always had a deep impact on me. It's on the same level as catching that first whiff of wet soil once the rain hits the ground . . . petrichor, I think it's called. I used to write a lot about rain clouds and how amusing I found it that my dad would take out the biggest soup pot (a 16-quart!) immediately after those clouds blocked the sun. . . . But it seems that I am my father's child. This soup is the first thing that I want when I'm ill, sad, cranky, or cold. It makes everything better. Maybe Dad felt the same about the soup that he made and shared with all the neighbors on our block. In fact, as soon as those closest to our house caught a whiff of the spices and onions cooking, they'd send their kids over with Tupperware containers to be filled once the soup was done.

My soup is a simpler version of my dad's, with a few aromatics, everyday brown lentils, and berbere, a rich Ethiopian blend of fragrant spices that adds just enough depth and heat to awaken the senses. It yields considerably less soup than my dad's but still enough to share with your neighbors.

2 tablespoons extra-virgin olive oil

1 large yellow onion, chopped

1 celery stalk, chopped

½ red bell pepper, finely diced

8 garlic cloves, minced

1 teaspoon kosher salt, plus more to taste

1½ tablespoons smoked paprika

1 tablespoon berbere

2 teaspoons dried parsley

2 teaspoons ground coriander

1 pound dry brown lentils, sorted

2 quarts Chicken Stock (page 259) or low-sodium chicken broth

3 whole cloves

1 fresh bay leaf

FOR SERVING (SEE NOTE)

1 cup plain Greek yogurt

Grated zest and juice of 1 lemon

Extra-virgin olive oil, for drizzling

Chopped fresh parsley, for garnish

1   In a large Dutch oven, heat the oil over medium heat. Once the oil is hot, add the onion, celery, bell pepper, garlic, and salt, and cook, stirring occasionally, until the onion is light golden and soft, 5 to 8 minutes. Add the smoked paprika, berbere, dried parsley, and coriander, and cook, stirring often, until the spices are fragrant, about 2 minutes. Add the lentils, stock, cloves, and bay leaf.

2   Reduce the heat to medium-low and cook, covered, stirring occasionally, until the lentils are very tender, 30 to 5 minutes. Remove and discard the bay leaf.

3   TO SERVE, ladle the soup into bowls, and top each with a dollop of yogurt, some grated lemon zest, and lemon juice. Drizzle each bowl with olive oil and scatter with chopped fresh parsley.

Note

While you can enjoy this soup as is, I highly recommend a slice of Sun-Dried Tomato & Olive Buttermilk Quick Bread (page 209) on the side. When I can find them, roasted merguez sausages placed on top are a welcome treat.

Haricots Verts with Burst Tomatoes & Cannellini Beans

Serves 4 as a main, 6 as a side Call it a side dish or a warm salad, this is such a simple way to add color to any plate. It's loosely inspired by a nineties three-bean salad, a dish that I never quite felt enthusiastic about due to the grayish hue of the canned green beans that my mom used. In this recipe, I add fresh haricots verts, the thinner version of regular green beans with a more robust flavor. To preserve their bright green color, it's essential to cook them in generously salted water, and just long enough until crisp-tender. I top the vibrant beans with a flavorful duo of cherry tomatoes and canned cannellini beans, two staples in my kitchen. If you're wondering about the anchovies, it's not a typo. They add great depth of flavor as they melt into the roasted tomato juices and olive oil, forming a delicious sauce that I spoon over the finished dish. Half of the time, nobody can put a finger on what the secret ingredient is, but there's never any leftovers.

2 tablespoons extra-virgin olive oil

2 tablespoons red wine vinegar

2 anchovy fillets, minced

1 large garlic clove, minced

½ teaspoon kosher salt, plus more for the boiling water

½ teaspoon freshly ground black pepper

2 pints whole cherry tomatoes

1 (15-ounce) can cannellini beans, drained and rinsed (see Notes)

1 pound haricots verts, tough ends trimmed

Torn fresh basil leaves, for garnish (optional)

1   Preheat the oven to 400°F with a rack in the center position.

2   In a large bowl, stir together the olive oil, vinegar, anchovies, garlic, salt, and pepper. Add the tomatoes and cannellini beans, toss to coat, then transfer to a rimmed sheet pan. Roast until most of the tomatoes have burst and the beans are warmed through, about 25 minutes.

3   Meanwhile, fill a large pot two-thirds of the way with water, and bring to a boil over medium-high heat. Once the water gallops, add a generous amount of kosher salt (I use 1 tablespoon for every 4 cups of water). Add the haricots verts and cook, stirring occasionally, until bright green and crisp-tender, 6 to 7 minutes. Drain and transfer to a serving plate.

4   Spoon the tomatoes, beans, and any juices on the sheet pan over the haricots verts. Garnish with torn fresh basil leaves, if desired, and serve immediately.

Notes
Use any variety of canned beans that you prefer, or replace the beans with cooked dried chickpeas—they definitely hold their shape better. In the summer, freshly shucked corn is an equally delicious substitute for the beans, especially when served with seafood dishes like grilled shrimp or seared tuna.

I think many of us can relate to the very, very grayish green beans that graced our plates as kids. Well, that is, if you're an elder millennial or above, like me. Nothing was worse than hearing my dad say, "Eat your vegetables,'" knowing that they looked so sad. That's why I prefer this method for cooking haricots verts that I picked up from America's Test Kitchen that ensures even, bright green beans. If you've let yours go for too long, chop them up finely, then add a generous amount of fresh lemon juice and olive oil, and season with salt.

Cabbage, Kale & Brussels Sprouts with Nutmeg

Serves 6   Cabbage sometimes gets a bad rap, but I have always loved this humble cruciferous vegetable in all its forms. Versions of this side dish appear in many cultures throughout the world, from Jamaican cabbage with Scotch bonnet peppers to Southern fried cabbage with bacon and a touch of sugar to tame any bitterness. Here, I steam and gently fry the cabbage in butter with kale and Brussels sprouts for a nutritious boost, then season with nutmeg and lots of black pepper—spices that form the cornerstone of many old-school South African recipes. It's a simple side that balances any stew or meat dish. Some good choices include the Miso-Braised Pork Shoulder (page 172), Birthday Beef Cheeks with Preserved Lemon Gremolata (page 139), or Kimchi-Braised Lamb Shanks (page 179). I prefer to cook these brassicas right before the main is done so that the warm butter coating the leaves is glossy at serving.

4 tablespoons salted butter

1 medium yellow onion, chopped

1 small red bell pepper, chopped

4 garlic cloves, minced

1 medium green cabbage (about 2 pounds), cored and chopped

2 cups chopped kale leaves (stems and tough ribs removed)

2 cups shredded Brussels sprouts

¼ cup water or low-sodium chicken broth

1 teaspoon coarsely ground black pepper

½ teaspoon kosher salt, plus more as needed

⅛ teaspoon freshly grated or ground nutmeg

In a large saucepan, melt the butter over medium heat. When the butter starts to foam, add the onion, bell pepper, and garlic, and cook, stirring occasionally, until the onion is translucent, about 2 minutes. Add the cabbage, kale, Brussels sprouts, and water, and cook, covered, until the cabbage is almost translucent and has lost some of its volume, 3 to 4 minutes. Sprinkle in the pepper, salt, and nutmeg, and cook, stirring occasionally, until the cabbage is tender and lightly caramelized around the edges, 6 to 8 minutes. Serve warm.

Secret Ingredient Potato Salad

Serves 8   There's this saying in South Africa: A can of condensed milk can repair broken hearts. Oftentimes, our parents would stick a spoonful in our mouths after a fall from a bicycle or skinned knee, both to calm the nerves and stop the crying. I myself have been caught taking a spoon to the condensed milk can on numerous occasions. My husband, DJ, never says anything because he knows how I feel about it. It's part of my culture!

This South African–style potato salad uses, you guessed it, a few spoonfuls of condensed milk. It balances the acidity of the mayonnaise and is always a hit at family barbecues. When I make it for my American family or new friends here, people ask: "Who made the potato salad?" And although that question can sometimes be seen as a negative, in my case, it's because they enjoy it and want the recipe! The idea of adding condensed milk to potato salad might seem strange at first, but it isn't a large amount, and combined with the crispy, salty bacon, red onion, and pickles, it works wonderfully. Try it with the Crispy Grilled Lamb Chops with Fresh Chakalaka Salad (page 176), Oven-Baked Gochujang Ribs (page 168), or alongside any of your favorite grilled foods.

2½ pounds russet potatoes, peeled and cut into 1-inch cubes

2 tablespoons kosher salt, plus more for seasoning

½ cup good-quality mayonnaise (I like Sir Kensington's; see Note)

¼ cup buttermilk

¼ cup finely chopped red onion

2½ tablespoons sweetened condensed milk

1 tablespoon Dijon mustard

2 tablespoons finely chopped kosher dill pickle (not dill pickle relish)

1 tablespoon chopped fresh parsley

1 teaspoon medium-grind black pepper

3 strips crisp-cooked bacon, chopped, divided

¼ cup pickle brine

1 tablespoon finely chopped fresh chives

1   In a large pot, combine the potatoes and the salt with enough water to cover the potatoes by 1 to 2 inches. Cook over medium-high heat, partially covered, until the potatoes are fork-tender, 12 to 15 minutes.

2   Meanwhile, in a large serving bowl, combine the mayonnaise, buttermilk, red onion, condensed milk, mustard, chopped pickle, parsley, pepper, and half of the bacon, stirring until fully combined. Taste the dressing and add salt, if needed.

3   Drain the potatoes over a large colander in the sink. Pour the pickle brine evenly over the hot potatoes. Let cool slightly, then transfer to the dressing. Toss to coat, then sprinkle with the remaining bacon and the chives. This potato salad is best when served warm immediately but can be kept at room temperature for up to 1 hour. If making it ahead of time, refrigerate for up to 1 day, then remove it from the refrigerator 1 hour before serving.

Note

Instead of the mayonnaise you can use ½ cup plain Greek yogurt combined with 2 tablespoons of fresh lemon juice.

Triple Truffle–Roasted Fingerlings

Serves 2   Let me start by saying that I used to harbor a reverse snobbery about truffles. As a budding young cook, I watched chefs on television shave truffles over all manner of dishes and wondered why the fuss. Was it really worth the significant investment to acquire said fungi? Later in life, when I dined at restaurants, I always avoided any menu item that mentioned truffles based on principle alone. As a poor kid I grew up with frugality in mind, so I considered luxuries like caviar or truffles unnecessary and pretentious— until I sampled truffle fries in Vegas. Once I got a hit of the oaky, nutty, hard-to-put-a-finger-on-it flavor of truffle, I thought about it constantly. Now, I keep a little collection of truffle salts, oils, or other "fancy" ingredients I spot when traveling, just like Nigella. They are a gift to myself to use in special recipes that I once shunned, like these crispy roasted fingerling potatoes, which get a double dose of the prized delicacy from truffle oil and truffle salt. They are a mild obsession, frankly. Sometimes, I take the potatoes to another level and dip them in a truffle mayo sour cream, and part of me wonders if my preference for mayo with potatoes is a lingering trace of my Dutch heritage. Thankfully, you don't have to sell a kidney for truffle-based products these days, and can easily find myriad options online. You just never know until you try.

POTATOES

1½ pounds fingerling or baby Dutch potatoes, uniform in size and halved lengthwise

2 tablespoons extra-virgin olive oil

1 teaspoon garlic powder

½ teaspoon truffle salt

½ teaspoon freshly ground black pepper

1 tablespoon truffle oil (see Note)

1 tablespoon finely chopped fresh parsley

TRUFFLE SOUR CREAM DIP (OPTIONAL)

½ cup sour cream

2 tablespoons truffle mayonnaise

1 tablespoon fresh lemon juice

1 teaspoon chopped fresh chives

1   Preheat the oven to 425°F with a rack in the center position. Line a rimmed sheet pan with parchment paper.

2   In a large bowl, toss the potatoes with the olive oil, garlic powder, truffle salt, and pepper. Arrange the potatoes, cut side up, in a single layer on the prepared sheet pan. Roast until golden brown and crispy, 35 to 40 minutes.

3   If desired, while the potatoes roast, in a small serving bowl, stir together the sour cream, truffle mayonnaise, lemon juice, and chives until well combined. Refrigerate until ready to serve.

4   Once the potatoes are roasted, transfer to a large serving bowl, then drizzle with the truffle oil and sprinkle with the parsley. Serve immediately with the sour cream dip, if desired.

Note

When it comes to truffle oil, reading the ingredient list truly matters. For the best flavor, look for oils derived from natural ingredients and avoid those containing words like *truffle flavor*, *essence*, or *aroma*. I prefer Sabatino truffle oils.

eight

SWEETS

Grandma's Rose-Scented Chocolate Birthday Cake

Serves 8   On our birthdays, my grandmother Rose always made it her mission to bake us a very special chocolate cake. It was layered with strawberry jam and heavily decorated with a rather firm chocolate frosting, fancied up by running the tines of a fork all over to create a ridged pattern; the final flourish was a crowning of glacé cherries on top. She'd transport the cake to our house in a cream and orange cake carrier that once belonged to my great-grandmother. This treasured vessel that held countless baked goods in its lifetime was always proudly displayed high up on her 1950s refrigerator, waiting its turn for another chocolate cake. It was a blessing to receive such a thoughtfully made birthday cake from Grandma, and when she passed away while I was writing this book, I knew I had to include a chocolate birthday cake recipe. Unlike Grandma's towering cake that served twelve people very easily, mine is a more modest two-layer cake. I flavor the jam filling with rose water, inspired by the legacy of my grandma Rose, who often spritzed herself with rose perfume. This recipe recognizes her dedication to celebrating every moment.

CAKE

1 cup all-purpose flour

1 cup sugar

2 tablespoons unsweetened Dutch-processed cocoa powder

1 tablespoon baking powder

1 teaspoon instant espresso powder

¼ teaspoon kosher salt

1 cup warm water

¼ cup vegetable oil

2 large eggs, at room temperature

1 teaspoon pure vanilla extract

CHOCOLATE GANACHE FROSTING

½ cup heavy whipping cream

1 (4-ounce) semisweet chocolate bar, roughly chopped

4 ounces cream cheese, softened

JAM FILLING

⅓ cup strawberry jam (marionberry jam is amazing if you can find it)

2 teaspoons rose water

1 cup fresh berries (I like raspberries, blackberries, and quartered strawberries), for decorating

1   TO BAKE THE CAKE, preheat the oven to 350°F with a rack in the center position. Grease a 9-inch round cake pan and line the bottom and sides with parchment paper.

2   In a large bowl, combine the flour, sugar, cocoa powder, baking powder, espresso powder, and salt and whisk together until blended. Pour in the warm water and stir, scraping down the sides and bottom of the bowl until no lumps remain. Whisk in the oil, eggs, and vanilla until fully combined and the batter is even in color. Pour into the prepared cake pan and cook until a toothpick or cake tester inserted in the center of the cake comes out clean, 25 to 30 minutes. Transfer to a wire rack to cool for 10 minutes, then invert the cake, remove the parchment paper, and let cool completely.

3   TO MAKE THE GANACHE FROSTING, microwave the cream in a microwave-safe bowl on high for 45 seconds or until hot. Add the chocolate and stir until the chocolate is completely melted and smooth. Transfer to the bowl of a stand mixer with the whisk attachment in place and let cool completely. Add the cream cheese and mix on high speed until the frosting is fluffy and uniform in color, about 1 minute. Set aside.

continues on page 234

4   MAKE THE JAM FILLING: In a small bowl, stir together the jam and rose water until well combined.

5   ASSEMBLE THE CAKE: Carefully cut the cake in half horizontally into two layers using a serrated knife or a level wire cake cutter. Spread the jam mixture all over the cut side of the bottom layer, then cover with the top layer, cut side down. Slather a thick layer of ganache frosting over the top and decorate with the berries.

Notes

The cake itself can be baked 1 day ahead of time, filled with jam, and stored in an airtight container at room temperature. Frost and decorate the cake when you're ready to serve. Adding the jam gives it time to seep into the cake. I promise it's very good.

MICROWAVE METHOD: This cake can also be cooked in the microwave oven! Pour the batter into a 9-inch round microwave-safe cake pan, and microwave on high power for 10 minutes, or until a cake tester inserted in the center of the cake comes out clean. All microwaves vary, so if the cake isn't ready, continue to microwave at 2-minute intervals until the cake tester comes out clean. Transfer the cake to a wire rack to cool completely before proceeding with the recipe.

Scones with Lemony Mascarpone & Jammy Strawberries

Makes 8 scones   Depending on your location, you might call them biscuits or shortcakes, but I've always known these buttery baked goods as scones. They graced the cake table on special occasions, like christenings or birthdays, and were served open-face a few different ways: slathered with butter, heaped with a generous grating of savory Gouda cheese, or piped with an old-fashioned ring of whipped topping around a pool of canned strawberry jam.

After getting married I found myself wanting to carry on the special-occasion scone tradition for friends and family here. Instead of the whipped topping, I now adorn the scones with lemon-curd-swirled mascarpone and juicy Louisiana strawberries with a touch of jam for sweetness. They're a great breakfast, dessert, or teatime treat any day.

SCONES

3 cups self-rising flour, plus more for dusting

1 tablespoon sugar

1½ teaspoons baking powder

1 teaspoon grated lemon zest

½ teaspoon kosher salt

1 stick (½ cup) unsalted butter, cubed and chilled

1 cup buttermilk, plus 2 tablespoons more, if needed

½ teaspoon pure almond extract

1 large egg, whisked

LEMONY MASCARPONE

1 cup mascarpone cheese

¼ cup store-bought lemon curd

1 tablespoon fresh lemon juice

JAMMY STRAWBERRIES

2 cups fresh strawberries, roughly chopped (or 12 ounces mixed berries)

¼ cup strawberry jam

1   TO MAKE THE SCONES, preheat the oven to 425°F with a rack in the center position. Line a sheet pan with parchment paper.

2   In a large bowl, whisk together the flour, sugar, baking powder, lemon zest, and salt until fully combined. Add the butter, and use two butter knives or a pastry cutter to mix it in until the flour resembles fine bread crumbs. Use a wooden spoon to make a well in the center, then pour in the 1 cup buttermilk and the almond extract. Stir until a dough forms. If the mixture looks dry, stir in the remaining buttermilk, 1 tablespoon at a time. Tip the dough onto a lightly floured work surface, and fold it over two to three times until it comes together. Do not overwork the dough or the scones will become tough. Pat the dough into a ¾-inch-thick disc. Use a 2½- to 3-inch biscuit cutter to cut out rounds, bringing the scraps together to cut out a total of eight rounds. (If you don't have a biscuit cutter, use a sharp knife to cut squares. Using something like a glass or a jar will "seal" the edges and prevent the scones from rising.)

3   Place the scones about 1½ inches apart on the prepared baking sheet, and brush the tops with the whisked egg. Bake until risen and light golden brown on top, 15 to 18 minutes.

4   Meanwhile, in a medium bowl, combine the mascarpone cheese, lemon curd, and lemon juice. Stir until fully incorporated and smooth.

5   TO MAKE THE JAMMY BERRIES, in a medium bowl, gently stir the strawberries with the jam until fully coated.

6   Let the scones cool completely before slicing them in half horizontally. Transfer to a serving platter, then top each half with 1 tablespoon of the lemony mascarpone and 1 tablespoon of the jammy strawberries. Alternatively, serve the scones with the ricotta and berries in separate small bowls for everyone to help themselves.

Fun Twist

The fruit and jam can be swapped out as the seasons change—try fresh peaches tossed in apricot preserves during peach season, or go all out with dulce de leche, sliced bananas, and whipped cream for extra-indulgent banoffee pie–inspired scones.

SCONES
WITH LEMONY
MASCARPONE
& JAMMY
STRAWBERRIES,
235

A Cup of Tea with Bubbles, for Luck

Serves 4   On Sundays, my mother prepared a pot of English tea to set on the cake table, a sideboard in the living room specifically for the purpose of displaying cakes or treats. "You need to starch those doilies," says my grandmother to my mom, disapproving of the way her crocheted handiwork looks under the dessert. My mom rolls her eyes and says, "These are modern times," then starts pouring the piping-hot milky beverage into thin-lipped teacups. When the teapot gets too low, Grandma proclaims, "Pour it higher! The week is only just starting, so we need lots of bubbles for luck!"

This story and method of pouring a humble cup of tea has remained with me all these years, and I find it a fitting addition to the last chapter in this book. Enjoy any of these homey desserts with a sweet cup of tea with lots of bubbles, for luck.

4 English breakfast tea bags

1 quart boiling water (see Note)

½ cup milk

Sugar, for serving

In a large teapot (more than 1-quart), combine the tea with the boiling water and let steep until you can smell it from the other side of the room, 3 to 4 minutes. Add the milk and cover the teapot. Pour the tea into cups from a height of at least 6 inches so that lots of bubbles form. Serve immediately at the table where your guests are gathered, with sugar on the side.

Note
Boil slightly more than 1 quart of water, then use the excess to rinse your teacups before pouring the tea. This will cleanse and warm the cups, keeping your cup of tea hot for longer.

Soetkoekies

Makes 3½ dozen cookies   During my last year at Stellenbosch University, I spent time with some grandmothers on the banks of a river as part of the necessary field experience for my degree in social work. My professors emphasized the importance of healthy emotional detachment from those we worked with, but the women, who lived in the small community of Jamestown, South Africa, had tugged on my heartstrings. To witness their appalling living conditions, often thin-metal shacks with only river rocks holding their roofs in place, gave me pause for thought. I was there to foster community-building, but somehow proposing that we do crafts, or bake cookies in the local church kitchen seemed pointless to me. How would it improve their current circumstances, or make their futures better? Many of the women raised their grandchildren, and during the voluntary hour spent with me, I could tell they were anxious to return home to check on their charges. There might've been more that I could've done, like arranging for childcare or involving their grandkids, but funding was limited and nobody cared what a young social work student had to say about fundraising. So, we continued and made crafts, sewed clothes, and visited around the riverbank. Now that I'm older, I realize that just acknowledging their space in the world, that they were not alone, might have buoyed these incredible ladies. They kept returning to spend time with me, and at the end of that year, when I graduated, we wept and embraced as we said goodbye.

These are the traditional and somewhat old-fashioned sugar cookies that we baked together in that community kitchen. Because of those remarkable ladies, who have since passed on, I developed a soft spot for the elderly, and for these heritage recipes passed down to me from the women in my life. My grandmother taught me to bake them in large batches for the holidays, with sprinkles and candied cherries cut up into tiny pieces because the container purchased needed to "stretch." Each *soetkoekie* only got a smidgen of cherry on top, and when those and the sprinkles ran out, we resorted to raisins. The ones with raisins were considered the "ugly ducklings" and the last to leave the cookie jar, not just for their appearance but for their bitter flavor after baking. My wonderful mother ate them in sacrifice so my sisters and I could enjoy the best of the batch. That's what moms do.

These hopeful, daisy-shaped cookies have provided generations of women in my family with something sweet to eat in our moments alone, and in our moments with those who needed us.

5 cups all-purpose flour

5 teaspoons baking powder

½ teaspoon kosher salt

½ pound unsalted butter, softened

2 cups sugar

3 large eggs

2 teaspoons pure vanilla extract

2 tablespoons lukewarm water, if needed

11 candied cherries, halved

Sprinkles

1   In a large bowl, whisk together the flour, baking powder, and salt.

2   In a stand mixer with the paddle attachment in place, cream the butter and sugar at medium-high speed until pale and fluffy, 2 to 3 minutes. Add the eggs, one at a time, beating to blend after each addition, until evenly incorporated. Add the vanilla, then tip in the combined flour, 1 cup at a time, beating at low speed to incorporate after each addition, until the dough is firm but not dry. If the dough looks too dry, add 1 to 2 tablespoons of lukewarm water, and mix until incorporated.

3   Tip the dough out onto a clean work surface, and gently knead by hand until no floury spots remain. Divide the dough into two equal pieces, flatten each one into a 1-inch-thick disc, then wrap each with plastic. Refrigerate for 30 minutes, and remove 1 disc before preheating the oven.

4   Preheat the oven to 350°F with a rack in the center position. Line two large rimmed baking sheets with parchment paper.

5   Place the disc of dough between two sheets of parchment paper, and roll to ⅛-inch thickness. Use a 3½-inch cookie cutter to cut out shapes, and gently transfer each one with a spatula to the prepared sheet pans, spacing the cookies about ½ inch apart. Bring any scraps of dough together, and repeat rolling between fresh sheets of parchment paper and cutting out shapes until the dough is used up. Gently press a candied cherry half into the center of half of the cookies, and pat the remaining cookies with sprinkles. Bake until golden around the edges and cooked through, 8 to 10 minutes. Repeat with the remaining disc of refrigerated dough.

6   Let the cookies cool on a wire rack. Store any leftover cookies in an airtight container at room temperature for up to 1 week.

Chocolate Coconut Nutella Sandwich Cookies

Makes 16 sandwich cookies These chocolate and coconut cookies are a riff on my favorite South African teatime treat, Romany Creams. I usually bring a box or two of the store-bought stuff back to America with me simply because of nostalgia, but they are gone within a few days and then I rely on my homemade recipe to get me through another year. My version replaces the melted milk chocolate that typically sandwiches the cookies together with Nutella, and how can you go wrong with that?

8 tablespoons unsalted butter, softened

½ cup sugar

1 teaspoon pure vanilla extract

¾ cup unsweetened finely shredded coconut (see Notes)

1 cup all-purpose flour

2 tablespoons unsweetened Dutch-processed cocoa powder

½ teaspoon baking powder

⅛ teaspoon kosher salt

½ cup Nutella or other chocolate-hazelnut spread

1   Preheat the oven to 350°F with a rack in the center position. Line a large baking sheet with a silicone baking mat or parchment paper.

2   In a stand mixer with the paddle attachment in place, cream the butter, sugar, and vanilla on medium-high speed until pale yellow and fluffy, 2 to 3 minutes. Add the shredded coconut, followed by the flour, cocoa powder, baking powder, and salt. Mix until the dough comes together, 2 to 3 minutes.

3   Measure 1 teaspoon (0.5 ounce, if weighing on a scale) of dough at a time and roll into a ball using your palms. Place on the prepared baking sheet and flatten slightly to about ½ inch thick. Press the tines of a fork on the surface of each cookie, to make a crisscross pattern and "roughen" them up. This gives them more texture.

4   Bake the cookies for 10 to 12 minutes, until they are just set. They will continue to crisp as they cool. Place them on a wire rack to cool completely, then spoon ½ teaspoon of the Nutella onto each flat side of half of the cookies. Top them with the remaining cookies, flat side down, to sandwich them. Store in an airtight container for up to 5 days.

Notes

Most shredded coconut you find at American supermarkets is coarser than the kind I use for these cookies. You can either buy finely shredded coconut at Indian grocery stores, or run the coarser coconut through the food processor until very fine.

These cookies can be made up to 2 months ahead and stored in an airtight container in the freezer. Thaw for at least 30 minutes at room temperature. They are particularly nice in the winter months when sweeter cravings hit. Dunk them in a hot cup of coffee just like we do in South Africa.

Classic Malva Pudding
with Bourbon Whipped Cream

Serves 8   This golden brown pudding cake takes less than an hour from start to finish. I like to think of it as a mash-up between British sticky toffee pudding and Mexican tres leches cake, because of the caramel flavor and sweetened milk sauce poured over right as the spongy cake comes out of the oven. Malva pudding is the kind of dessert that you could make on a whim with ingredients like fruit preserves and evaporated milk from the pantry, and I grew up eating it mostly on Sunday afternoons. If you visit any South African restaurant or take a flight to the mother city, it's likely to be on the menu either served with a British-style ambrosia custard or whipped cream. I like to top my malva pudding with bourbon whipped cream because it adds a pleasant bitter note to the otherwise sweet cake. For freshness and crunch, serve it with seasonal fruit like pears in the fall, or cherries in the summer, and toasted nuts (hazelnuts are great!), but it doesn't necessarily ask for anything when served as-is, either.

MALVA PUDDING

1 tablespoon unsalted butter, softened, plus more for greasing

1 cup sugar

1 large egg, at room temperature

1½ tablespoons apricot preserves

1 cup whole milk

1 tablespoon apple cider vinegar

1 teaspoon pure vanilla extract

1 cup all-purpose flour

1 teaspoon baking soda

½ teaspoon baking powder

½ teaspoon kosher salt

BOURBON WHIPPED CREAM

1 cup heavy whipping cream

1½ tablespoons bourbon

SAUCE

1 (12-ounce) can evaporated milk

2 tablespoons pure maple syrup

1 teaspoon pure vanilla extract

FOR SERVING (OPTIONAL)

Fresh seasonal fruit

Toasted hazelnuts

1   TO MAKE THE MALVA PUDDING, preheat the oven to 350°F with a rack in the center position. Butter a 9-inch square or round baking dish or 10-inch pie dish.

2   In a large bowl, whisk together the sugar, egg, apricot preserves, and the 1 tablespoon butter until pale yellow and smooth, 1 to 2 minutes. Add the milk, vinegar, and vanilla extract and whisk until well combined. Add the flour, baking soda, baking powder, and salt and whisk until a runny batter forms.

3   Pour the batter into the prepared baking dish and bake until a skewer inserted in the middle comes out clean and the top has a deep golden brown color, 30 to 35 minutes. (The cake should not jiggle when you remove it from the oven.)

4   MEANWHILE, TO MAKE THE BOURBON WHIPPED CREAM, in a large bowl, combine the heavy cream and bourbon and whisk together until soft peaks form. Chill until ready to serve.

5   MAKE THE SAUCE 10 MINUTES BEFORE THE MALVA PUDDING COMES OUT OF THE OVEN: In a small saucepan, combine the evaporated milk, maple syrup, and vanilla extract, and cook, stirring occasionally over medium-low heat until the sugar is dissolved. Reduce the heat to low, cover and keep warm until the cake is ready.

6   Pour the sauce over the malva pudding immediately after it comes out of the oven. It may look like too much liquid initially, but give the sauce a few minutes to settle in. The malva pudding will come away from the edges of your baking dish slightly once you pour the warm evaporated milk over, this is normal.

7 TO SERVE, dollop each portion with bourbon whipped cream, and serve with fresh fruit and toasted hazelnuts, if desired.

8 Let any leftover cake cool in the baking dish (sans whipped cream on top), then cover with plastic wrap and refrigerate for up to 3 days. Rewarm in the microwave or a 350°F oven before serving.

Creamsicle Pannekoek

Makes 8 pannekoek (about 4 servings)

South African *pannekoek*, also known as *pannenkoek* in the Netherlands, are thin crepe-like pancakes that can be enjoyed for breakfast or dessert depending on how you serve them. The old-fashioned pannekoek of my childhood is typically sprinkled with cinnamon sugar and served with lemon wedges, but this Creamsicle-inspired spin is incredibly refreshing and a welcome update to the original. Fresh orange slices take the place of lemon juice while nutmeg in the cinnamon sugar boosts the complexity. A ricotta topping laced with vanilla and fresh orange juice seals the Creamsicle deal. Ricotta con latte, a milkier ricotta cheese with a mild, pleasantly sweet flavor, is definitely worth seeking out for this recipe. It has a next-level creaminess compared to its regular counterpart, but mascarpone cheese is a notable stand-in, if unavailable.

When I speak with other South Africans who now live overseas, pannekoek always comes up as the one dish that most of us continue to prepare in our new home countries. They are essential, pretty affordable to make, and equally as dear to us as the fluffy version is to many families here in the US.

PANNEKOEK
2 large eggs

1 cup whole milk

½ cup water

1 teaspoon fresh lemon juice

1 teaspoon pure vanilla extract

1 cup all-purpose flour

1 teaspoon baking powder

¼ teaspoon kosher salt

¼ cup vegetable or sunflower oil (or substitute almond oil)

SPICED SUGAR
3 tablespoons sugar

2 teaspoons ground cinnamon

½ teaspoon ground nutmeg

RICOTTA TOPPING
1 (8-ounce) cup ricotta con latte

3 tablespoons fresh orange juice

1 tablespoon pure maple syrup

1 teaspoon vanilla bean paste

FOR SERVING
2 medium oranges, peeled and thinly sliced

¼ cup loosely packed torn fresh mint leaves

1   TO MAKE THE PANNEKOEK BATTER, in a large bowl, combine the eggs, milk, water, lemon juice, and vanilla extract and whisk togetheruntil frothy, about 1 minute. Add the flour, baking powder, and salt and whisk until evenly incorporated. Finally, add the oil and whisk until the batter is smooth and has the consistency of heavy cream. Let the batter rest for 10 minutes at room temperature before cooking.

2   MEANWHILE, TO MAKE THE SPICED SUGAR, in a small bowl, combine the sugar, cinnamon, and nutmeg, stir, and set aside.

3   TO MAKE THE RICOTTA TOPPING, in a medium bowl, combine the ricotta con latte, orange juice, maple syrup, and vanilla bean paste and stir together until well blended and smooth.

4   TO COOK THE PANNEKOEK, heat a medium nonstick skillet over medium heat, and have a plate ready for the finished pannekoek. Briefly stir the batter to redistribute the ingredients. Add ⅓ cup of the batter to the skillet and carefully pick up the skillet, swirling until the batter coats the bottom. Cook the pannekoek until the bottom is golden brown, 45 to 50 seconds. Flip and cook for 10 seconds on the other side, then transfer to the plate. Sprinkle 1 teaspoon of the spiced sugar evenly over the top, and repeat this process with the remaining batter. It is okay to stack the pannekoek on top of each other on the plate; they will not stick together and the residual heat from each one will keep the others warm until you're ready to eat.

5   TO SERVE, fold each pannekoek into quarters or loosely roll each one, jelly-roll style, and divide among serving plates. Sprinkle with any remaining spiced sugar, top with a generous spoonful of the ricotta mixture and the orange slices, then garnish with the mint.

Butter Pecan Banana Pudding Cups

Serves 8   While I generally cook a lot of meals from scratch, I cringe a little at food snobbery. In this house, if I'm making dessert it should be quick and convenient because I'm not trying to open a bakery here. The goal is to give people exactly what they love, save for dietary considerations and things of that nature, of course. Sometimes, shortcuts are absolutely fine, and I stand by my version of banana pudding, made with boxed vanilla pudding and vanilla wafers (you know the ones!). I first tasted banana pudding on my wedding day, made from scratch by a family friend, Miss Penny; my husband, DJ, could not stop raving about it. Then, I discovered the easy version online and put my own spin on it so that it's semi-homemade. I like this version better, and so does the whole family. When taking this approach, it makes sense to jazz up the quality of the other ingredients. I toast pecans in salted grass-fed butter with crushed vanilla wafers, then layer the sweet and salty duo with bananas and French vanilla pudding mix enriched with cream cheese. Maple-sweetened heavy cream whipped with pure vanilla bean paste tops the banana pudding cups, and it's garnished with store-bought praline pecans for crunch. I'm famous (in my house) for this humble banana pudding dessert. These are the best kind of sweets.

1 stick (8 tablespoons) salted butter

1 (11-ounce) box vanilla wafers, such as Nilla wafers, crushed

1 cup pecans, roughly chopped

2 (3.4-ounce) packages French vanilla instant pudding mix

3 cups cold milk (I prefer whole milk, but any kind will do)

1 cup sweetened condensed milk

8 ounces cream cheese, softened

4 medium bananas

2 tablespoons fresh lemon juice

1½ cups heavy whipping cream

1 tablespoon pure maple syrup

1 teaspoon vanilla bean paste

½ cup praline pecans, for serving (optional)

1   In a large skillet, melt the butter over medium heat. When the butter starts to foam, add the crushed wafers and pecans, and cook, stirring often, until the pecans are toasted and the wafers have absorbed the butter, 3 to 4 minutes. Remove the skillet from the heat and set aside to cool completely.

2   In a stand mixer with the whisk attachment in place, combine the pudding mix, milk, condensed milk, and cream cheese, and mix on medium speed until very smooth and thickened, about 2 minutes.

3   Peel and slice the bananas into ¼-inch-thick coins. Drizzle with the lemon juice.

4   In eight (6-ounce) cups or glasses, layer the cooled wafer and pecan mixture, pudding, and bananas, dividing evenly, until you've used up all the ingredients, finishing with a layer of the pudding. I usually get about two layers per cup.

5   In a stand mixer with the whisk attachment in place, combine the heavy cream, maple syrup, and vanilla bean paste, and mix on medium speed until soft peaks form, about 2 minutes. Spoon the whipped cream on top of the pudding and top with the praline pecans, if using. Serve immediately.

Cinnamon Custard Tart (Melktert)

Makes 1 (12-inch) tart (about 8 servings)

Like the Italian dessert *torta della nonna*, this traditional South African tart is pastry cream–based, but whereas the Italians add pine nuts, we dust the finished *melktert* with a rather generous amount of ground cinnamon. Some people who aren't familiar with the dessert claim that it's too much, but it totally works and doesn't overpower the delicate milky flavor of the filling. My mother is a master at whipping it up at the last minute, and it often appears on the cake table out of nowhere to savor with a cup of rooibos tea. So many South Africans can instantly recognize the rich buttery aroma of melktert. It is the one recipe that we all seek out during the holidays, especially expats here in the United States.

PASTRY

Nonstick baking spray

2 cups all-purpose flour, plus more for dusting

2 teaspoons grated fresh orange zest

1 teaspoon baking powder

½ teaspoon kosher salt

1 stick (½ cup) cold unsalted butter, cubed

½ cup sugar

1 teaspoon pure vanilla extract

2 large eggs

CUSTARD FILLING

½ cup sugar

2 large eggs

3 tablespoons cornstarch

1 teaspoon vanilla bean paste (or 1 teaspoon pure vanilla extract; see Note)

¼ teaspoon ground nutmeg

2 cups whole milk

2 tablespoons cold unsalted butter, cubed

1 teaspoon cinnamon, for serving

1 TO MAKE THE PASTRY, preheat the oven to 350°F with a rack in the center position. Spray a 12-inch tart pan with a removable bottom with baking spray.

2 In a food processor, combine the flour, orange zest, baking powder, and salt, and pulse until just combined, 3 to 5 seconds. Add the butter, sugar, vanilla, and eggs, and pulse until the dough comes together, about 1 minute.

3 Tip the dough out onto a lightly floured surface and gently press it together by hand until a solid dough forms. Using a rolling pin, roll the dough into a 14-inch round about ⅛ inch thick. Carefully roll the dough onto the rolling pin and center it over the prepared tart pan, then unroll from one end to the other. Press the dough into the tart pan and remove any overhang from the edges of the pan. Using a fork, prick a few holes into the bottom of the pastry. Place a sheet of parchment paper on top and pour in some dry beans. Bake until the pastry is light golden brown, 10 to 12 minutes.

4 MEANWHILE, TO MAKE THE FILLING, in a medium bowl, combine the sugar, eggs, cornstarch, vanilla bean paste, and nutmeg and whisk together until smooth. Set aside.

5 In a medium saucepan, heat the milk over medium heat until small bubbles start to form around the edges, 3 to 4 minutes. Remove from the heat, pour about ¼ cup into the egg mixture, and whisk until completely smooth, 1 to 2 minutes. (This is to temper the eggs so they don't scramble.) Add the tempered eggs to the warm milk in the saucepan and cook over medium-low heat, whisking rapidly until the filling thickens and can coat the back of a spoon, 5 to 8 minutes. Stir in the butter until melted and remove from the heat. Pour the filling into the pastry, and dust with the cinnamon. Let cool for 15 minutes before slicing, and refrigerate any leftovers in an airtight container for up to 3 days.

Note

I use vanilla extract in the pastry and vanilla bean paste in the filling because I like the way the flecks look in the custard.

No-Churn Green Tea
Ice Cream Cones

Serves 4 to 6   During our courtship, DJ took three-hour-long bus rides from his military duty station in Uijeongbu to visit me in Wonju, oftentimes right after physical training was done and just in time for the last bus leaving the station. He used to tell me about the ice cream–filled waffles that he purchased from vendors just outside of the subway station in Seoul, sometimes his only option for food in a rush so that he could make his connecting transfer to me on time. We were inseparable in those nine months that we dated in Korea. Green tea ice cream is an important part of our beginning, and I've made an easy version (that doesn't require an ice cream maker) for him here in Mississippi for almost a decade. I scoop it into a retro waffle cone with sprinkles and a maraschino cherry on top. The ice cream is also delicious served alongside any kind of melon.

GREEN TEA ICE CREAM
1 cup sweetened condensed milk

2 tablespoons food-grade matcha (green tea powder)

1 teaspoon pandan extract (optional; see Note)

2 ounces cream cheese, softened

2 cups heavy whipping cream

FOR SERVING
Waffle cones

Sprinkles (optional)

Maraschino cherries (optional)

1   TO MAKE THE ICE CREAM, in a blender, combine the condensed milk, matcha, and pandan extract, if using; blend until bright green and no dark green streaks remain, about 10 seconds. Set aside.

2   In a stand mixer with the whisk attachment in place, beat the cream cheese on medium speed until smooth, about 15 seconds. Scrape down the sides of the bowl, add the heavy cream, and whisk on medium-high speed until soft peaks form, about 1½ minutes. Spoon in half of the condensed milk and whisk to combine. Using a rubber spatula, fold in the remaining condensed milk until even in color.

3   Spoon into an 8 × 4-inch loaf pan or 1-quart container. Cover tightly with plastic wrap and freeze for at least 6 hours, up to 5 days.

4   TO SERVE, remove the ice cream from the freezer 10 to 1 5 minutes before scooping to let it soften a bit. Scoop into waffle cones, then top with sprinkles and cherries, if desired.

Note
Pandan extract is a concentrated green paste with flavor extracted from pandan leaves, the same ingredient that gives Thai sticky rice its signature tropical, floral taste. Here, the extract is used to give the ice cream depth of flavor and brighten up the color (some matcha powders used on their own will yield a less appealing mint green, grayish hue). Find pandan extract online or at your local Asian grocery store.

Honey-Do Banana Bread

Makes 1 (9 x 5-inch) loaf (about 8 servings)

For a while when we were little, we lived in the Eastern Cape province of South Africa on the edge of a dense forest teeming with monkeys. Our yard was cut off from the forest by a wall and what must've been a cluster of twenty tall banana trees. In the evenings, the monkeys would come and eat avocados, bananas, and other fruit that Mom cut up and arranged on the wall. It was fun to watch them, until the day Aretha, who was five years old at the time, decided to play with matches. She struck one and flung it into the banana grove. Within minutes there was smoke, then flames, then falling bunches of hot bananas. Panicked, and only seven at the time, I started to fill our beach buckets with water in a futile attempt to quell the flames so that our parents wouldn't find out. The fire truck arrived within a few minutes but we weren't overjoyed; we started crying based solely on the look on Dad's face. We knew what it meant. Thankfully, the banana grove survived, but we learned a valuable lesson that day.

This banana bread is DJ's favorite, and I'm reminded of the above story without fail every time I bake it for us. When he realizes that the warm, not-too-sweet snack is on the horizon, I've noticed more zealous attempts to complete my honey-do list in the spirit of reciprocity. That's why it's been dubbed Honey-Do Banana Bread here at home.

Butter, for greasing

2 cups all-purpose flour, plus more for dusting

2 large ripe bananas (see Note)

1 large egg, at room temperature

½ cup whole milk

⅓ cup vegetable oil

1 teaspoon pure vanilla extract

1 cup sugar

½ cup chopped pecans

1 tablespoon baking powder

1 tablespoon flaxseeds

1 tablespoon poppy seeds

¼ teaspoon kosher salt

1   Preheat the oven to 350°F with a rack in the center position. Butter and flour a 9 × 5-inch loaf pan and set aside.

2   In a large bowl, use a whisk to mash the bananas, then whisk in the egg, milk, oil, and vanilla extract.

3   In a medium bowl, stir together the 2 cups flour, the sugar, pecans, baking powder, flaxseeds, poppy seeds, and salt until well combined. Add the dry ingredients to the wet, and stir with a wooden spoon until the flour is just combined.

4   Pour the batter into the prepared loaf pan and bake until a skewer inserted into the middle of the loaf comes out with little to no crumbs attached, about 1 hour. Remove from the oven and tip the banana bread out onto a wire rack to cool before slicing.

Note

For a better-tasting banana bread, make sure that your bananas are ripe, brown in spots, almost falling apart when peeled. If your bananas aren't very ripe, bake them on a rimmed sheet pan at 350°F for 5 minutes or until the skin is dark brown, then allow to cool before using in the recipe. My mother always mashes the bananas first, letting them sit for 30 minutes at room temperature to get darker for a richer flavor.

Amarula Dom Pedro

Serves 2   At the foot of the Drakensberg mountain range in the little town of Wellington where I grew up sits a very old distillery that has sent the smell of whiskey and sherry wafting through our neighborhood for many generations. During bottling season every year, those captivating aromas would linger, and start to give us crazy ideas about making mixed drinks like this Dom Pedro, South Africa's beloved boozy milkshake.

Halfway between a drink and a dessert, Dom Pedros can be found on most restaurant menus throughout the country, especially at bigger steakhouse chains because they provide a delicious cool reprieve after enjoying savory foods like steak. They are usually served in stemmed wineglasses with chocolate syrup and shavings of dark chocolate on top, and this sight alone has made any guest I've served it to here very, very happy. My husband, DJ, orders it almost immediately after we touch down in South Africa for our December vacations, with an extra shot of whiskey to get into that holiday spirit. The kind of whiskey that you use doesn't matter too much, but the key to the flavor is Amarula, a cream liqueur from South Africa. I often substitute Kahlúa coffee liqueur here because Amarula is harder to find stateside. If you're willing to go the extra mile, I highly recommend seeking out the Amarula for that authentic South African flavor.

2 cups softened vanilla ice cream

½ cup whole milk

½ cup Kahlúa coffee liqueur or Amarula cream liqueur (see Note)

¼ cup whiskey

2 tablespoons chocolate syrup

FOR SERVING (OPTIONAL)

Whipped cream

1 tablespoon grated semisweet chocolate

2 maraschino cherries with stems attached

1   In a blender, combine the ice cream, milk, liqueur, and whiskey. Blend until creamy and smooth, about 1 minute.

2   Divide the chocolate syrup between two stemmed wineglasses, swirling it around to create an interesting pattern on the walls of the glasses. Pour the Dom Pedro into the glasses and top with some whipped cream and the grated chocolate, if desired. I like to add a maraschino cherry on top for the aesthetic. Serve immediately.

Note

Amarula liqueur is made from the fruit of the African marula tree. Elephants are known to snack on the fruit, and that's interesting because the marula tree is also known as the elephant tree. If you were wondering why there's an elephant on the label of the bottle, that's why.

nine

BASICS

Creole Seasoning

Makes ½ cup   This blend takes its inspiration from the classic Creole seasoning, Tony Chachere's, that I was first enthusiastically introduced to by my mother-in-law, Iscinova, during my first week here in America. I do love the original and use it often, but my version is more herb-forward and includes a few nontraditional add-ins, like dried thyme and smoked paprika, two of my favorite flavor boosters.

2 tablespoons garlic powder

2 tablespoons onion powder

1 tablespoon kosher salt

1 tablespoon smoked paprika

2 teaspoons paprika

1 teaspoon dried thyme

1 teaspoon dried oregano

1 teaspoon dried basil

½ teaspoon cayenne pepper

½ teaspoon freshly ground black pepper

In a jar, combine the garlic powder, onion powder, salt, smoked paprika, paprika, thyme, oregano, basil, cayenne pepper, and black pepper. Close the jar and shake to combine. Store in a cool, dry place for up to 1 month.

Easy Pickled Red Onions

Makes 1 (8-ounce) jar   There aren't many cookbooks these days that don't include a recipe for pickled onions and with good reason. They are the easiest way to give any recipe that special touch and do so much to revive leftovers as well. I like to use white balsamic vinegar for my pickled onions because it has a well-rounded flavor and subtle sweetness, making it less sharp than the usual white distilled vinegar. The Smoky Chicken–Topped Sweet Potatoes (page 107), Steak & Cheesy Egg Breakfast Tacos (page 194), and Lamb Meatballs for a Mezze Platter (page 183) all benefit from their brightness. Use them anywhere you would pickles—on hot dogs, burgers, or even chopped in a tuna salad.

1 small red onion, halved lengthwise and thinly sliced

¼ cup white balsamic vinegar

Pack the onion tightly into an 8-ounce jar or container. Add the vinegar, close with the lid, and shake to coat. Let sit for 15 minutes before using. Refrigerate any remaining pickled onions for up to 2 weeks.

Preserved Lemons

Makes 2 quart-size jars   Unique ingredients, spices, and foods in pretty packaging are the first things I seek out when traveling because they always reignite my passion for cooking. Preserved lemons have been the best addition to my pantry because they add a salty, almost floral pop of flavor to recipes that need a little something extra. Before I started making my own, I first learned about the mellow, yet intensely lemony Moroccan condiment from my friends Ron and Leetal Arazi of New York Shuk. If you'd rather buy a jar, they offer both whole preserved lemons and paste of very high quality, available online. If, however, you do find yourself with some lemons, preserving them at home is a straightforward process. The only caveat is that they need at least three weeks until they're ready, but once the lemons are preserved they keep for up to six months in the refrigerator.

Once I make a batch, I can use the preserved lemon rind in myriad ways: minced in a vinaigrette, pureed to stir into stews, and sliced and stuffed into a whole chicken before roasting. Either homemade or store-bought, they're a must in recipes, like the Pasta with Scallops & Lemony Garlic Butter (page 93), Mustard & Marcona Almond–Dressed Eggs (page 55), and Wild Rice Bowls with Roasted Beets, Goat Cheese & Preserved Lemon Drizzle (page 215).

12 medium lemons, quartered

1 cup coarse sea salt

1 tablespoon whole black peppercorns

2 fresh bay leaves, lightly crushed

2 fresh rosemary sprigs

2 quart-size canning jars, sterilized (see Note)

1   In a large nonreactive bowl, combine the lemons with the salt and massage by hand until the lemons are fully coated and their juices start to seep out. Add the peppercorns, bay leaves, and rosemary sprigs, then use a muddler or potato masher (or even a heavy jar) to press down on the lemons until they release as much juice as possible.

2   Divide the lemons, peppercorns, and herbs among the jars, and pour over any juice left in the bowl, using the muddler to immerse the lemons in liquid. Close the jars and store in a cool, dry place for 1 week, then refrigerate for up to 6 months. The lemons are ready when the salt in the jars is fully dissolved and the liquid is clear, about 3 weeks. To use, remove a lemon from the jar with a fork, and scrape away the flesh (it's much saltier than the preserved rind). Thinly slice the rind, or use the flat side of a knife to puree it before using in a recipe.

Note

Here's an easy method to sterilize canning jars without having to deal with a large pot of boiling water: Preheat the oven to 250°F with a rack in the bottom position. Wash your jars in hot soapy water, rinse and dry thoroughly, then place them on the bottom oven rack for 25 to 30 minutes. Use grip tongs or oven mitts to remove the jars, and fill them while still warm before closing with nonreactive lids.

Chicken Stock

Makes 4 quarts (16 cups) If buying chicken stock is more convenient for you, by all means, please do so. When pressed for time you can't beat the convenience of good-quality store-bought stock, but once a month I find myself with a few pounds of trimmed bones after butchering some chickens. It's a nice way to use every part of the bird and add natural flavor to special meals, so if you have the time and chicken to use, consider making a batch.

3 pounds chicken carcass, backs, and necks

2 large carrots, scrubbed and halved crosswise

1 celery stalk with leaves, roughly chopped

1 large yellow onion, unpeeled and quartered

8 garlic cloves, peeled

6 fresh parsley stems

2 fresh thyme sprigs

2 teaspoons black peppercorns

1 fresh bay leaf

Kosher salt

1 In a large, heavy-bottomed stockpot, combine the chicken, carrots, celery, onion, garlic, parsley, thyme, peppercorns, and bay leaf; add enough water to cover by 1 inch. Bring to a boil over medium-high heat without stirring. This could take as long as 15 minutes. Once bubbles start to form around the edges of the pot, reduce the heat to low, and use a slotted spoon to skim off any grayish foam that rises to the surface. Continue to simmer, uncovered, skimming off foam every 30 minutes and adding more water if needed to keep the ingredients covered, for about 3 hours.

2 Place a colander over a large, deep bowl or another stock pot, set in the sink. Carefully and slowly, strain the chicken stock, stopping once the bowl is full. Use another bowl, if needed, until all the stock is strained. Discard the solids in the colander.

3 Ladle the stock into storage containers and let them cool completely. Cover and refrigerate for up to 3 days or freeze for up to 6 months.

Everyday Gochujang Sauce

Makes 1 cup This is my go-to sauce when preparing any Korean or Korean-inspired recipes using gochujang, a fermented red chili paste that grew on me so much over the course of my time teaching there. I use it as a glaze in the Salmon Ssam Feast (page 82) and for my Oven-Baked Gochujang Ribs (page 168) and to drizzle over anything requiring a boost of flavor. The slight tang of rice vinegar and sweetness of maple syrup perfectly balances the spice, and makes it pourable enough to keep in a squeeze bottle in the refrigerator. I think it's the perfect addition to rice with slices of fried Spam, eggs, a drizzle of toasted sesame oil, and roasted seaweed for dinner on busy weekdays. It makes a great dip for fresh cucumber spears, carrot sticks, or crisp-tender broccoli, and can be used as a spread on your favorite sandwiches. Since gochujang varies widely in terms of flavor and heat level, it may be necessary to try a few brands before settling on one that you prefer. In my opinion, gochujang from Korea's Sunchang county has a nice depth of flavor. You can find it called out on the labels on containers at your local Asian grocery store, or online. The better the quality of the gochujang, the more delicious this sauce will be.

½ cup mild gochujang

¼ cup plus 2 tablespoons rice wine vinegar

¼ cup pure maple syrup

2 garlic cloves, minced

2 teaspoons soy sauce

2 teaspoons toasted sesame seeds

In a glass jar, stir together the gochujang, vinegar, maple syrup, garlic, soy sauce, and sesame seeds until fully incorporated and smooth. Use right away, or cover and refrigerate for up to 5 days.

Easy Mak Kimchi

Makes about 1 quart (6 to 8 servings) My first encounter with kimchi, the tangy, spicy staple of Korean food, was as a twenty-one-year-old in South Korea. I was fresh off the plane from South Africa and anxious to start my new job as an English teacher there. I faced many challenges in that first year but sought solace in my students. I was loved by the children and, in turn, appreciated by their parents, who, during the winter solstice, would hand me large containers of kimchi as gifts. At first the taste was new, too different, and strong for my still undeveloped palate . . . but then subtle differences in flavor started to become more apparent as I worked my way through the varying containers in the refrigerator. Briny, deep, umami, crunchy, acidic, spicy, intense, and some without chili, even refreshing. The gifted kimchi often kept me from going hungry, and now, if I had to choose my final meal on this Earth, I would unequivocally include it on the side. It's become a comfort food, of sorts.

I was later picked up by one of the other schools full-time, where I remained and taught for five wonderful years as an English cooking teacher. Intrigued by the process of kimchi making, I relished any advice given by school cooks who would allow me to join them in preparing more than eighty whole heads of napa cabbage at a time when kimchi-making season began. The first step was salting the cabbage in huge plastic tubs outside where they would sit in the winter sun until wilted, sometimes a few days. Next, the wilted cabbage was rinsed and massaged with a bright red seasoning paste of gochugaru, thickened starch, salted shrimp or fresh oysters, and various vegetables. The fresh kimchi would be packed into large clay jars and left to ferment, then shared between everyone and stored in special kimchi refrigerators indoors to use throughout the year. It was a sight to behold, and an experience that I'll not soon forget.

When my husband and I first settled here in Mississippi, kimchi was not an everyday ingredient in supermarkets like it is now, and neither were some of the ingredients to make it. I craved it endlessly, and even tried to buy some from a local Korean couple who happily shared, but eventually I started making my own. While mostly sticking to the advice I was fortunate enough to receive from so many Korean cooks, this recipe is also partly inspired by the formidable YouTuber Maangchi and her Emergency Kimchi. Watching her prepare kimchi with green cabbage, the only kind available during her travels in Mexico, allowed me to think about flexibility when it comes to recipes. There are a million variations out there now. While I still believe that the best kimchi is in a big tub at H Mart or from someone with years of experience and "seasoned hands," as my mother would say, those aren't options for me.

This is my at-home kimchi, a base recipe with a short ingredient list that you can customize to your liking. Whereas kimchi made with heads of napa cabbage is typically salted and fermented whole or quartered, I chop the cabbage first, in the style of "mak kimchi" or chopped kimchi. The pear can be swapped out for an apple, or even pineapple, a tip I picked up from a fellow kimchi-loving friend, Lucia! Bromelain, an enzyme found in fresh pineapple (the same enzyme that gives you tongue tingles when eating the fresh fruit) helps the fermentation process significantly, and I especially like using pineapple when planning meals with kimchi that benefit from a tropical twist, like the Miso Pulled Pork Nachos (page 63).

1 medium head napa cabbage (2 to 3 pounds), outer leaves and stem trimmed, cut into 2-inch pieces

¼ cup kosher salt

1 small yellow onion, roughly chopped

1 small ripe pear or apple, peeled, cored, and quartered (or ⅓ cup chopped fresh pineapple)

4 large garlic cloves

1 (1-inch) piece fresh ginger, peeled and roughly chopped

3 tablespoons fine gochugaru

2 tablespoons fish sauce

2 teaspoons sugar (optional)

4 green onions, cut into 1-inch pieces

1   Place the cabbage in a large colander and rinse under cold running water while tossing a few times by hand to wash away any impurities. Drain, but do not completely dry the cabbage, as the moisture will help the salt to penetrate the leaves quicker. Add the salt to the cabbage in the colander and gently massage into the pieces. Cover the colander with a clean kitchen towel and let sit at room temperature (I leave mine in the sink) until the cabbage is wilted and bends easily without snapping when folded, 3 to 4 hours. Rinse the cabbage thoroughly under cold running water to remove excess salt then drain. Transfer to a large bowl.

2   Meanwhile, in a food processor, combine the onion, pear, garlic, ginger, gochugaru, fish sauce, and sugar, if using. Pulse, scraping down the sides and adding a few tablespoons of water if needed, until a chunky paste forms, about 2 minutes.

3   Transfer paste to a medium bowl and fold in the green onions. Massage this seasoning paste into the cabbage.

4   Pack the kimchi and any liquid in the bowl tightly into jars and loosely close with the lids. Place the jars on a plate to collect any overflow as the kimchi ferments, and set in a cool, dry place until bubbles start to form, about 3 days in hotter weather or up to 1 week in colder weather. Taste the kimchi. It should be slightly sour and leave a tingle on your tongue once fermented. When you're happy with the flavor, wipe the jars and seal tightly. Let the kimchi continue to ferment in the refrigerator for another 3 days, opening the lids once daily to release any trapped gas. Use within 6 months, and always check that the cabbage is mostly submerged in liquid when storing to prevent it from spoiling.

Note

Aged kimchi has a more intense flavor than fresh kimchi, and has been fermented for at least 3 to 6 months. To achieve this in a shorter amount of time, I let my fresh kimchi sit on the counter for at least 2 weeks before refrigerating. As long as the kimchi is submerged in liquid, and is kept covered in a clean container, it should be fine. I also make my next batch of kimchi when I'm halfway through my current supply, so that I always have fresh and aged on hand.

Garlic Peri-Peri Sauce

Makes 1 cup   This spicy sauce of chilis, lemon, olive oil, and garlic is Portuguese in origin, and was first made with chilis cultivated in Mozambique, a former Portuguese colony just off the east coast of South Africa. Over time, this all-purpose hot sauce became part of the South African culinary identity, and we adopted the sauce as *peri-peri*, which translates to "chili-chili" in Swahili. Some people prefer to purchase the sauce already bottled, and you can, too, as it's become widely available in American grocery stores in recent years. However, before this was possible, I created this less fiery homemade version with easier-to-find ground spices (instead of tracking down fresh African chilis) and maple syrup to balance out the flavors. This sauce is used in multiple ways throughout this book: Garlic Peri-Peri Roast Chicken (page 124), Shrimp Tacos with Peri-Peri Yogurt Sauce (page 95), and Creamy Chicken Livers on Toast (page 127). I recommend doubling the batch to keep in your refrigerator.

¼ cup extra-virgin olive oil

¼ cup fresh lemon juice

1 tablespoon apple cider vinegar

1 tablespoon pure maple syrup

6 large garlic cloves, roughly chopped

2 teaspoons onion powder

2 teaspoons smoked paprika

1 teaspoon peri-peri chili powder or any other chili powder, such as ancho, chipotle, or Kashmiri (or substitute 1 fresh red chili)

1 teaspoon crushed red pepper

1 teaspoon dried oregano

1 teaspoon kosher salt

In a food processor, combine the oil, lemon juice, vinegar, maple syrup, garlic, onion powder, smoked paprika, chili powder, crushed red pepper, dried oregano, and salt. Process until completely smooth, about 3 minutes. Pour into a jar, then store in the refrigerator until ready to use, up to 4 weeks.

Miso Tahini Sauce

Makes ½ cup   This sauce is inspired by *ssamjang*, a Korean condiment usually prepared with doenjang (a fermented soybean paste), gochujang (a fermented red chili paste), garlic, green onions, and chili. My version combines white miso (a Japanese stand-in for the doenjang) and gochujang with tahini, which adds the nuttiness from sesame seeds that I like but with more flavor. I use the miso tahini sauce as a condiment for meats and vegetables, like the Spicy Pork & Eggplant Lettuce Wraps (page 181) and as a dipping sauce for summer rolls, and raw vegetables like cabbage, cucumber, and carrot sticks.

2 tablespoons white miso

2 tablespoons smooth tahini

2 tablespoons finely chopped green onion

1 tablespoon finely diced green chili (seeded for a milder sauce)

1 tablespoon pure maple syrup

2 teaspoons gochujang

1 teaspoon minced garlic

1 teaspoon low-sodium soy sauce

In a jar or small container, stir together the miso, tahini, green onion, chili, maple syrup, gochujang, garlic, and soy sauce until well combined. The sauce can be used immediately, and any leftovers refrigerated for up to 1 week.

Yogurt Feta Sauce

Makes 1½ cups   This is my very favorite all-purpose sauce because it contains a healthy amount of creamy feta cheese, and lifts the flavor of any dish that you serve it with. Try it with the Lifesaving Lemon Pepper Chicken Patties (page 109), Lamb Meatballs for a Mezze Platter (page 183), or in place of the plain yogurt on the Greek(ish) wedge (see page 132). It's also a great dipping sauce for fresh vegetables, and can be thinned out with more lemon juice or water to make a delicious dressing for any simple green salad.

½ cup plain Greek yogurt

½ cup mayonnaise

6 ounces feta cheese, crumbled

2 tablespoons fresh lemon juice (from 1 medium lemon)

1 tablespoon chopped fresh dill

1 tablespoon chopped fresh parsley

1 tablespoon chopped fresh chives

1 garlic clove, minced

1 to 2 teaspoons honey, to taste (optional)

In a jar combine the yogurt, mayonnaise, feta, lemon juice, dill, parsley, chives, and garlic and stir together. Taste, and stir in honey, if desired. The sauce will keep in the refrigerator for up to 5 days.

District Six Apricot Chutney

Makes heaping ½ cup   This chutney is what I use in my mom's older recipes instead of buying Mrs. H.S. Ball's Peach Chutney, a well-known South African peach and apricot chutney made with dried fruits, vinegar, and spices. I adapted it from District Six Instant Chutney from the book *Cass Abrahams Cooks Cape Malay: Food from Africa* by Cass Abrahams. Here, I use apple cider vinegar instead of brown malt vinegar. When I left for South Korea, I managed to convince my mom to give me her dog-eared copy that contained many of our family's favorite recipes. The pages are stained with butter and flour, and the photographs tell a story of postapartheid life in the segregated Cape Town neighborhood known as District Six. The chutney is a staple in most homes, but it was not always as easy to find or affordable for home cooks without means. Cape Malay cooks have always been known for their resourcefulness, and this cheat chutney was probably first stirred up to replace the store-bought version as well.

½ cup apricot preserves

3 tablespoons apple cider vinegar or white balsamic vinegar

1 garlic clove, minced

½ teaspoon red pepper flakes

½ teaspoon ground cumin

½ teaspoon kosher salt

In a jar, combine the apricot preserves, vinegar, garlic, red pepper flakes, cumin, and salt. Close with the lid and shake vigorously until well combined. Use immediately, or store in the refrigerator for up to 1 week.

Small-Batch Stovetop Peach & Apricot Granola

Serves 4 (about 4 cups) Ours is not a household where cereal is on the menu often, much less as a breakfast during the week, but there are times when we crave a bowl of not-too-sweet granola with tart Greek yogurt or unsweetened almond milk. This small-batch granola makes just enough for us to enjoy a few times before we inevitably get tired of cereal and move on to more savory meals. It is made in a skillet on the stovetop for speed and convenience, with a variety of seeds for added crunch and nutrition, and dried peaches and apricots for natural sweetness. During the harvest season in South Africa, our old wooden kitchen table was home to a big bowl of ripe peaches and apricots. Naturally, I love the combination. Granola is highly personal, so play around with combinations that you love. In the fall, try dried apples, cranberries, and pecans. In the winter, we love a mix of dried dates, figs, and hazelnuts. Serve it with your favorite yogurt, plant-based milk, or use it as a topping for your next fruit crisp.

1 tablespoon coconut oil

2 cups old-fashioned rolled oats

½ cup sliced almonds

⅓ cup mixed seeds, such as poppy, flax, and hulled sunflower and pumpkin seeds

⅓ cup pure maple syrup

2 tablespoons light brown sugar

½ teaspoon ground cinnamon

¼ cup finely chopped dried peaches

¼ cup finely chopped dried apricots

1 In a large skillet, heat the oil over medium heat. Add the oats, almonds, and mixed seeds, and toast, stirring often, until the oats are lightly golden and fragrant, about 5 minutes. Transfer to a large rimmed sheet pan, and spread into an even layer. Reserve the skillet.

2 Pour the maple syrup into the skillet, then add the brown sugar and cinnamon. Cook over medium heat, stirring, until the sugar is dissolved and the syrup is bubbling, about 1 minute. Drizzle over the toasted oats, then add the dried peaches and apricots. Using a silicone spatula or tongs, carefully toss until fully coated and sticky. Let cool for 10 to 15 minutes (the granola will crisp up as it cools), then break up any larger clumps, and store in an airtight container at room temperature for up to 1 week. I like to store mine in the freezer (where it'll keep for up to 6 months) so that it's extra-cold and crunchy when ready to serve.

ACKNOWLEDGMENTS

Baie dankie (ˈbɑɪə ˈdɑŋki)
Interjection (*Afrikaans*)
thanks a lot; thank you very much

Writing a cookbook is no small task, and for a procrastinator like me, it took a lot of helpers to put together what you hold in your hands today. A thousand thank-yous to everyone who supported this dream of mine! Somehow, we've made it to the end!

To the brilliant team at Simon Element and Simon & Schuster, thank you for rallying behind this book and for working diligently to make it the best that it could be. Justin Schwartz, I couldn't have asked for a better editor than you. You believed that my story was worth telling from the start and championed this project with tremendous enthusiasm. I'm eternally grateful for all the hand-holding, plus your flexibility and patience while I figured things out.

Stacey Glick, my literary agent at Dystel, Goderich & Bourret, who approached me one day with this wild idea that I, too, could be an author. Thank you for your support and encouragement!

Susan Choung, your trained eye, edits, research, and advice meant that I could rest easy when I needed to. Thank you for making sense of my writing, for your dedication to the manuscript, and for going above and beyond to see it through with me. I hope you love the finished product as much as I do.

To my husband, DJ, thank you for all the little (and big) sacrifices you made so that I could devote myself fully to this book. I know it wasn't easy but look what we did! I hope you're proud of what we've accomplished together. Here's to ninety-nine years old.

Bella Karragiannidis, I couldn't have done this without you. Thank you for putting your life on hold to come to Mississippi and for being as invested as I was in this process. Thank you for the beautiful photography sprinkled throughout these pages, and for the many late nights that you sacrificed without a second thought. Your creative direction and dedication to the integrity of this project was invaluable, and your belief in me kept me going. I'm so very proud to call you my best friend, forever.

Laura Palese, I'm so honored that you agreed to design this book. Your expertise and thoughtful touches took it to a whole new level, thank you!

Meredith Bradford at Staub USA, I can always count on you and your team. Thank you for your generosity when it came to the props.

Aliza Simons at Henry Street Studio, thank you for those brainstorm sessions early in the photography process and for offering to help.

I'm eternally grateful to my family, both by blood and by choice, who have been invested in the success of this book since the idea first popped into my head. Mom, you taught me how to cook and care for those around me. Your generosity and kindness laid the foundation for how I live now, and it's because of this that I'm able to express my love to others. Thank you, Aretha, Calvin, Kim, Peter, Daniel, Cameron, and Lily, for being there every step of the way. Deverie Gray Sr. and Iscinova Gray, thank you for welcoming me into your family and for showing this South African girl the ropes when it came to Southern food. Kristen Williams, thanks for helping during the early stages of testing! Many thanks to my neighbor Anna Smith for offering sound advice and brutal honesty when the burnout was real. Thanks for organizing all the ingredients, for sitting with me in the kitchen while I cooked, and for getting me out of the house from time to time! Kayla Wheeler, thank you for the positive energy that you injected into my days during a time when it would've made more sense for you to think of yourself. Thank you for fighting, thank you for surviving, and thank you for your fierce loyalty over the years.

And finally, a very special thank you to all of the Daley Plate supporters around the world. Your DMs, emails, phone calls, and encouragement kept me going. This book is for you.

INDEX